Praise for 11:11 The Time Prompt Phenomenon

"See 11:11 all the time? How about 333 or 444? These enigmatic time prompts or number sequences are the language of the universe, speaking to you all the time. But do you understand why they are so important, what they are trying to tell you, and how the brain actually processes numbers and number symbols? The answers to these and more questions will surprise you. This book covers the mysterious world of numbers and what they might be trying to tell us—individually, and collectively."

—Joshua P. Warren, TV personality and author of *Use the Force*

"Is it happening to you? You wake up at night, look at the clock, and notice that it is 11:11 p.m. It happens repeatedly, and you think it is a coincidence, but then you start to discover that it is happening to others all around the world, and you wonder. Reports of people noticing strange and repeated associations with the number eleven are on the rise, prompting theories connecting this phenomenon with the advent of the new Mayan calendar. But it's not just the number eleven that is showing up in people's lives; it is often accompanied by unusual events or profound insights. Mysterious numbers and strange sequences appear throughout the history of human experience. What do they mean? What secrets do they keep? Are these wake-up calls to a higher state of consciousness? In this fascinating new work, *11:11 The Time Prompt Phenomenon* will explore the mysteries of 11:11 and the many other ways in which numbers compose the very foundation of our reality."

—Atherton Drenth, author of *The Intuitive Dance*

"*11:11 The Time Prompt Phenomenon* is a splendid compilation offering insight into the spiritual and scientific aspects of numbers. As an intuitive medium and number enthusiast, I wholeheartedly believe that Spirit provides the perfect message at the perfect time via the perfect messenger, and many times these messages are in the form of numerical sequences. Fulfilling my own fascination with numbers, Marie D. Jones and Larry Flaxman's book is truly impressive and will leave you enthralled."

—Shelly Wilson, author of *28 Days to a New You, Connect to the You Within,* and *Journey into Consciousness*

"Get ready for a new appreciation of the mystical, magical world of numbers as Jones and Flaxman take you on a rollercoaster ride through the workings of the brain, the levels of mind and consciousness, even the deep and murky world of archetypes. The universe, God, angels, higher source, or whatever you choose to call it is speaking to you all the time via number sequences and synchronicities, but as the authors warn, you must pay attention to see and understand the messages. *11:11 The Time Prompt Phenomenon* covers every aspect of why numbers are the highest form of communication between our normal waking state and elevated levels of awareness that can help us live a better life."

—Kac Young, PhD, author of *The Art of Healing with Crystals*

"In this digital age, we are literally enveloped by numbers, and, not surprisingly, the eternal fascination with numbers is stronger than ever. Marie D. Jones and Larry Flaxman provide an invaluable primer on the intriguing history and meaning of numbers, the lore of mystical numerology, time synchronicities, sequences, ratios, codes, Pythagorean secret societies, sacred geometries, and much else. Absolutely a fascinating read guaranteed to leave you counting for more!"

—Robert M. Schoch, PhD, author and editor of books including *The Parapsychology Revolution* and *Pyramid Quest*

"*11:11 The Time Prompt Phenomenon* is a fun, fast-moving, informative discussion of numbers as both spiritual and scientific concepts and of the fundamental significance of numbers as they have been viewed throughout the ages of humanity. I recommend it as a thoroughly enjoyable read, after which you may never look at numbers the same way again."

—Laird Scranton, author of *The Science of the Dogon* and *Sacred Symbols of the Dogon*

"A beautifully written exploration of digital synchronicity and the sacred mysteries encoded in numbers. As someone who struggles with dyscalculia (numerical dyslexia), I appreciate how the authors explain complex mathematical concepts so that even a lay person like myself can understand them. Bravo!"

—Laurie Nadel, PhD, psychotherapist and author of *The Five Gifts*

"If you've ever seen repeated number sequences and wondered what they were trying to tell you, Jones and Flaxman offer a comprehensive guide to both the scientific and spiritual aspects of these mysterious time prompts. This is a wonderful book that will completely change your relationship with numbers and open your eyes to the powerful symbolism behind number patterns."

—Nick Redfern, author of many books, including *The Real Men in Black*

THE TIME PROMPT PHENOMENON

Mysterious Signs, Sequences, and Synchronicities

Marie D. Jones and Larry Flaxman

This edition first published in 2019 by New Page Books, an imprint of
Red Wheel/Weiser, LLC
With offices at:
65 Parker Street, Suite 7
Newburyport, MA 01950
www.redwheelweiser.com

Copyright © 2019 by Marie D. Jones and Larry Flaxman
All rights reserved. No part of this publication may be reproduced or transmitted in any form or by any means, electronic or mechanical, including photocopying, recording, or by any information storage and retrieval system, without permission in writing from Red Wheel/Weiser, LLC. Reviewers may quote brief passages. Previously published in 2009 by New Page Books, ISBN: 978-1-60163-047-6.

ISBN: 978-1-63265-167-9
Library of Congress Cataloging-in-Publication Data available upon request.

Cover design by Kathryn Sky-Peck
Interior by Timm Bryson, em em design, LLC
Typeset in Warnock Pro

Printed in the United States of America
IBI
10 9 8 7 6 5 4 3 2 1

To Mary Essa and Max

Acknowledgements

Marie and Larry would like to thank our agent, Lisa Hagan, for, well... everything. She is just the best. We would also like to thank Michael Pye for championing this book from the very beginning and bringing it to its new home at Red Wheel/Weiser. We so look forward to this new chapter with Michael and his team.

To our families, friends, followers, fans, and, most of all, to our kids, Max and Mary Essa—we thank you for all your support over the years!

Contents

INTRODUCTION
The Measure of Reality 1

CHAPTER 1:1
Wake-Up Calls and Codes of Consciousness 5

CHAPTER 2:2
This Is Your Brain on Numbers 23

CHAPTER 3:3
Sacred Sequences and Cosmic Codes 45

CHAPTER 4:4
Signs and Symbols 81

CHAPTER 5:5
Mystery Numbers 103

CHAPTER 6:6
Name, Rank, and Serial Number 119

CHAPTER 7:7
Synchronicity 133

CHAPTER 8:8
Just Six Numbers?   151

CHAPTER 9:9
The Trouble with Numbers   171

CHAPTER 10:10
Is God a Number?   183

CHAPTER 11:11
Why Numbers Matter   203

APPENDIX
Number Trivia and Anomalies   207

Bibliography   221

Introduction

THE MEASURE OF REALITY

"One day you will learn to appreciate numbers."

"Math will serve you well, just you wait and see."

"Everything comes down to a number or series of numbers, even if it isn't obvious."

How often have we heard such phrases, usually spoken by well-meaning parents, teachers, and college professors? In this age of instant gratification, we immediately receive answers via cell phone, calculators, and search engines. All of the work is done for us. In fact, some might argue that we don't even need to know math anymore! Why even balance your checkbook when it can be done automatically by nearly every online banking program or app? The world has changed, and our need to understand the numeric world has been drastically diminished.

It's a shame really, because there is magic and wonder in numbers . . . especially when they appear in distinct and repetitive patterns that suggest some deeper force is at work underlying the obvious and visible reality of our five senses. All over the world, people report seeing number patterns throughout their day, whether on digital clocks or restaurant bills, or even bus benches. Many see the same pattern and wonder, what is this trying to tell me? What is this numeric sequence saying?

There are those who see 1:11, 2:22, 3:33, and so on. 12:12. 12:34, and possibly the most popular and oft reported number sequence—11:11. If we did pay attention to our math teachers, we would have heard them say that numbers and number ratios are the language of our universe, and that if we were to someday be visited by some extraterrestrial civilization, they likely would not speak to us in English or Chinese or Dutch . . . but in the one language that is truly recognizable no matter what planet you come from. Numbers.

Now don't you wish you had paid more attention to cranky old Mr. Hodgkins in eighth grade math class?

Those who are enamored by and attracted to the world of mathematics know that underneath the algebra and geometry and calculus lessons is a world of complete and utter supernatural, creative, and generative power. Behind every great scientific discovery in physics, astronomy, and many other arenas, lies a series of equations that look Greek to most, but contain the alchemical ingredients for all of creation, from gaseous stars to asteroids, human life, and other biological forms.

Yes, science is filled with math and numbers, but so, too, is the world of spirit. As we moved past the enigmatic year of 2012, when so many people worried the world would end over a misinterpreted Mayan calendar, people reported seeing a particular sequence everywhere: 11-11. They pointed to the exact time of the winter solstice's arrival in December 2012. 11:11 GMT. They suggested it was not the end of the world at all, but the beginning of a new era of spiritual growth, transformation, and ascension.

Cut to so many years later, and we still live in a world of dichotomies. Good and evil, light and dark, peace and violence. Yet there is a sense of having ascended somehow into a greater understanding of the whole "as above, so below" way of looking at human existence. Today, thousands of people continue to see time prompts and sequences, most notably 11:11, but plenty of others, too, and more and more report the experience each year. Is it possible we are collectively being contacted by other "beings" such as angels, spirits, guides, hey—maybe even extraterrestrials? Is this their way of reaching out and getting our attention so that we will stop surfing the Internet, posting to social networks, *and pay attention?*

The idea of spiritual transformation is certainly not a new one. There is still considerable debate as to whether or not we are in the Age of Aquarius or have already moved through this era of positive change, both individually and collectively. But look around . . . talk to people . . . and even amidst the political chaos and ongoing strife, there is a growing sense of connectedness to our inner beings, to one another, and to the natural world around us.

It would be easy to say that people who report seeing these time prompts only ascribe personal meaning to them because it makes them feel good or that it is just the trick of a brain that loves to glom onto any kind of pattern it can find and make order out of a chaotic world. But what of the stories of synchronicities, magical and miraculous coincidences, and "aha" moments that people insist occur each time they look up and see "11:11" or "3:33"? Perhaps there is something more going on than just pure coincidence, more than just a noggin trained to notice only what it wants to notice.

Perhaps, there are messages and signals and information floating in the ether just waiting for us to lock on to them and allow them to help us live better lives. Perhaps it is our higher selves speaking to us in a way that gets us to notice amidst the many distractions tugging at our limited range of perception. Perhaps it is a doorway to transformation that, if entered, can lead humanity to higher ground.

Numbers and mathematics were once important to ancient philosophers and men and women of wisdom. They knew what we have forgotten. Yet those engaged in the most cutting-edge frontiers of scientific discovery have not forgotten. Right before his death in March 2018, legendary theoretical physicist Stephen Hawking wanted a particular equation on his gravestone. Known as the Hawking Equation, it's a mathematical expression of his greatest work into the makeup of black holes, specifically that black holes emit a glow known as Hawking Radiation. Not only did this equation allow us to understand more about black holes, but about the entire process of growth and change of our universe over time.

In the final days of his life on earth, Hawking was working on an attempt to solve the mystery behind whether or not parallel universes existed. He spent decades pondering this one question alone and worked over and over with mathematical ratios and equations to try to unlock the key to other realities and other worlds. He even published a paper before his death titled "A Smooth Exit from Eternal Inflation," explaining his theory on how current physics could indeed explain the existence of these other universes that exist alongside our own. Those who flocked online to read the paper had to have had a mathematical or physics background to make sense of it, but to Hawking, it was akin to a mystical, magical doorway to the possible. It will now be up to other brilliant minds to take on the challenge of finding absolute proof.

But for those who are grounded in this reality, yet have experienced the liminal—the threshold between above and below, life and death, this world and that, one level of conscious awareness and another—proof already exists. We are more than just bodies, and the spirit already knows what science is still struggling to crunch the right numbers on.

Chapter 1:1

WAKE-UP CALLS AND CODES OF CONSCIOUSNESS

"Last night as I pulled into my driveway, I looked down at my mileage and it read 11,111.1! Weird! Then [sic] I woke up this morning at 2:22 a.m.! This is just getting too weird! Those angels are working their magic!"

"I began seeing 1111 many years ago. I also see 111, 222, 333, and so on. Sometimes I'll wake in the middle of the night at exactly 1:11. These numbers have appeared on boxes, license plates, house numbers, friends addresses, phone numbers, totals at the grocery store."

"I woke up at 11:11 last night! I had only been asleep a short time! This morning I was outside with my granddaughter and she said she wanted to go in! Weird, she never wants to go in! So we went in and turned the TV on... I noticed that the time on the screen was 11:11! I love the little reminders... makes my day go so much better!"

11:11. 11-11. 1111. No matter what form it takes, the number sequence of four 1s is the most often reported "time prompt," or number sequence, in the world. Dating back to the 1970s, when new age groups spoke of the coming golden age of humanity, the "age of Aquarius" when we would come out of the shadows of the murky Piscean age and walk into the light of awakening, this particular number sequence has fascinated and enchanted thousands of people. The meaning behind it has been hotly debated, but suffice it to say, those who regularly experience it believe they are being "prompted" to wake up, pay attention, and get ready in body, mind, and spirit.

But ready for what?

Even as scientists insist that numbers are the universe's chosen form of language, and the age of technology exists around binary code, we have another side to us that recognizes these numbers on a whole different level. Human consciousness, which we still really don't know whether exists as part of the mind or outside it, appears to operate on its own "code," and communicates with higher levels of existence via the use of number patterns that speak to a deeper, archetypal collective unconscious. Meaning, our brains don't quite get it, but our spirits do.

In terms of 11-11, or 11:11, there are some unusual properties to think about right off the bat. According to *TimeandDate.com*, the number 11 is considered mathematically special because it is a primary number. When any string of 1s is multiplied by itself, it equals a palindrome. Let's try it:

11 X 11 = 121
111111 X 111111 = 12345654321
111111111 X 111111111 = 12345678987654321

Spooky, right? But does this mean anything other than some number sequences have really peculiar properties that seem to hold a higher intelligence within? Maybe.

11:11 THEORIES

The connection between 11:11 and other time prompts and number sequences has spawned numerous theories involving everything from angelspeak to codes of DNA and human consciousness, to mere pokes in the side from our dead relatives and ancestral spirits trying to get us to open our eyes, focus, and notice something. The significance of 11:11 is almost as varied as the people who see it on a regular basis!

Some of the more persistent and widespread theories suggest that the appearance of these numbers somehow portend that a window is about to open and you must consult with your guides, spirit or otherwise, as to whether or not you should go through it. According to Alanna Ketler in "What is the Significance of 11:11" on the Collective Evolution website, when you see this number sequence, you should stop and make a wish. The association of 11:11 and making a wish is a popular one, perhaps fueled by social networking where it seems to have gone viral. Memes and images abound encouraging people to make a wish every time they see this number pattern, even though finding the origin of this theory is somewhat impossible (Hollywood has taken notice, with a few 11:11-oriented movies).

The phenomenon of 11:11 is usually positively associated with ascension of the spirit and consciousness, so when we see this prompt, we are supposed to stop and take notice, be open to whatever sensations, thoughts, and feelings we have, and be receptive to the synchronicities that follow. But the same might be said for 3:33, or 12:12, right? If all this means is you should slow down and lift your consciousness, couldn't you do that anytime you want to? The same article goes on to state, "When you see 1111, whether on a clock, a license plate, your bank statement, or anywhere else, it's like a friendly little sign from your soul, source, higher self, God, or the entire universe—whatever you choose to call it—that everything is in alignment and you are exactly where you need to be, right here, right now." There is something extremely intriguing about this. The idea that we resonate more positively to certain numbers, words, and phrases over others is paramount to understanding why seeing four 1s turns us on both spiritually and mentally.

WHY 11:11?

11:11 is pure, symmetrical, and pretty to look at. The number one often refers to God, source, and creation. Numerologists claim the number 11 itself points to spirituality, revelation, enlightenment, idealism, and intuition, so maybe that is why this particular sequence has a more profound effect on us than 12:12 or 5:55 or 120021. Unless one of those other patterns has extreme personal significance, like the birthday of a child or an important street address, we generally don't perceive the same level of meaning that we see in 11:11. For those seeking more scientific proof of the importance of numbers, in the next chapter we will explore some of the reasons why our brains seem to love both symmetrical number sequences and numbers of all kinds.

In terms of spirit, any explanation can be ascribed some meaning when a number sequence or time prompt keeps showing up. Believe in spirit guides? That's them talking to you! Angels? Pay attention, they are guiding you! Twin Flames? The man or woman of your dreams is coming! Awakened consciousness? The time prompts tell you to get ready! It is all subjective and often based upon our own beliefs and perceptions, even our religious background or world view. A quick peek at any social networking site offers these explanations and more for the appearances of time prompts such as 11:11.

If you are of a religious bent, you may believe that the number 1 is a divine number representing the One, the All, or God. A non-religious person would look at the same number and suggest it represents a leader, or even the self. "Looking out for Number One." A depressed loner will look at the number 1 as representing a lonely state of existence, as in "One is the loneliest number." It is also the number of unity, wholeness, and completeness. Yet another person might say it is the number of solitude and being left to his/her own devices. Yet at the most objective level, based on its Proto-Indo-European root, the number 1 simply means there is only one of whatever it is that is being counted! In mathematics, it is simply a digit that comes after zero and before two.

Yet in complex mathematics, the number 1 becomes a dynamo that is involved in numerous ratios and equations and is one of the most critical base numbers there is, if not the most critical, to establishing measurement and quantity. Without the number 1, we would not have computers or algebra or physics or even the ability to distinguish an individual object out of a million other objects, similar or otherwise.

NUMBER VIBES

Aside from the mathematical importance, though, our spirits/minds resonate with the number 1, whether alone or doubled, as in 11, or symmetrical, as in 11:11, in a much different way. On a symbolic level, we feel it is a connection to a higher power or source, a God source if you will. We sense it has importance as a foundational building block to human life and even consciousness (even if we don't know the details behind it). We claim to feel a sense of resonance with the frequency the number sequence "gives off," based on our already scientific understanding of how important the number 1 is but added to our understanding that there is another side to our existence that goes beyond the mere physical.

Might the symmetry of 11:11 give us a sense of balance in a chaotic world? Does the appearance of this time prompt on our clocks and digital readouts remind us to balance our work life with our play life, our emotions with our thoughts, our masculine with our feminine qualities, our positive with our negative? If so, the appearance of this time prompt helps us to be more grounded and aware, even if there is no scientific basis for this kind of meaning. Who cares, if it works!

In "Spiritual Meaning of Number Eleven" from *Whats-Your-Sign.com*, the author states that "Those who recognize the spiritual meaning of the number Eleven in their lives are quite sensitive to vibrational frequencies matching these attributes listed." Those attributes include: calm, tact, balance, justice, kindness, equality. The article goes on to say that those who see elevens all the time are thoughtful and intuitive souls. Perhaps this explains why some people never see 11:11 or any other time prompt. They are not wired to do so or are not operating on the correct vibrational frequency to make the connection.

In "11:11. Is It Happening to You?" on *PowerofPositivity.com*, the author posits that our spirit guides, angels, or higher selves know how powerful the act of repetition is in driving home important wisdom and insights. "Our Spirit Guides, angels, or higher selves like to speak to us through various methods, such as playing a recurring song on the radio that may have special significance, answering a prayer, flipping to a certain page in a book we're reading, or even directing our attention to repeating numbers on a clock, or sign, such as 11:11." Then, as this happens to more and more people, who talk about it on social networks, it goes viral; soon there is a collective shift in consciousness and awareness as more people become aware of the same number sequence. The article goes on to say that the "turning of ages" began back on December 21, 2012, at 11:11 a.m., which, coincidentally, is the exact time the Winter Solstice began and continued to usher us into the Golden Age and out of the Dark Age. Ascended masters will come back to the planet to assist in our healing and growth (the return of ancient aliens perhaps?).

Therefore, seeing 11:11 means you are on the right path, and should stay put, stay focused, and listen for more guidance. Those familiar with 11:11 attest to the increase of synchronicities that happen when these time prompts appear, and that they are little pokes and prods reminding us to stay present enough to notice and process them. Otherwise, we miss ample opportunities for growth and ascension.

TWIN FLAMES

For some, that growth may come from finally meeting up with a twin flame. In "The Phenomenon and Meaning of 11:11: The Twin Flame Connection," on the Elephant Journal website, the number sequence may be telling us to pay attention to things that increase our soul's growth and to prepare for a life filled with things we may not have imagined possible. One of those things is the potential manifestation of our Twin Flame, or the unique soul connection we share with the person from whom our soul was separated when we came into this incarnation.

The concept of Twin Flames originated with the idea that before we were born, our souls were once made of two halves. When we incarnate upon this earth, we do so alone, and long to return to the "other half" of our soul if we can find that person in this lifetime. In order to do so, we must be spiritually ready for this "high level of comfort, intimacy, understanding of each other and a sense of peace—it's the feeling of returning home." The time prompts of 11:11 we see are markers along the path back to our Twin Flame, and reminders that we must be in a high vibration to meet and connect with them once more.

Seeing 11:11 means that we need to get ready, for our Twin Flame is nearby or about to make himself or herself known to us. Will we be in a state of present moment awareness to be able to recognize them, or focused on the regrets of the past or the anxieties of the future, and miss them altogether?

DNA AND NUMBERS

In a later chapter, we will delve into numerology, which ascribes particular characteristics to numbers using our names or dates of birth. Like astrology, it's all in the details and a number or letter has its own powerful meaning and its own vibration. Thus, the numbers or translation to letters in your name, or the numbers in your birthdate that add up to a "master number" can give you incredible insight into yourself, your future, and your dreams. More on that later.

Does the appearance of number sequences suggest something that might be encoded in our DNA? Could our genetic material have the key that goes into the lock that, when opened, reveals a true understanding of who we are and why we are here? Possibly. There are books about 11:11 being a doorway to another dimension, another reality, and another level of consciousness for those lucky enough to recognize the signs and heed them. A genetic revolution of sorts that makes us superhuman and able to operate on a whole new level. The number 11 can represent our twin strands of DNA, that when fully "activated" will trigger a new and higher vibrational frequency upon which our consciousness operates. 11:11 is the number of the shift that must occur to each one of us as individuals, but also to the whole of society to lift the planet out of darkness and into the light of a new conscious revolution. A Golden Age that will bring about greater spiritual awareness, peace, and compassion.

If indeed the number sequence of 11:11 is directing us toward a Golden Age, shouldn't we all be seeing it continuously? A possible answer to that could be that we must be aware and present to see the sequence. But really, how often do we busy, distracted humans spend in the present? We stress over the past. We stress over the future. We bury our heads in our computers and cell phones and gadgets, unaware of what is passing us by—if only we looked up and focused.

Spiritual awakening cannot occur to someone who is so trapped in the physical world and so focused on the non-spiritual. Perhaps seeing 11:11 now and then is a way to get more and more people to stop, look, listen, and find the guidance they need to play their own individual roles in the evolution of the planet and all its beings. Maybe it also serves as a way for us to "remember" why we are here and realign with our purpose by examining our thoughts, behaviors, and actions to see if they truly reflect who we are and hope to be.

ANGEL NUMBERS

Many people believe angels are behind these time prompts. It is a way for our angels and spirit guides to make us pay attention so that they can impart a message of wisdom or insight we need to hear. At first, we see a particular number sequence just once or twice, but soon we are seeing it everywhere, and we cannot help but pay attention to it. As we begin to ask ourselves what these signs might mean, it's important to stay open to what we are thinking and experiencing in the present moment and look for clues to decode the messages. Angels and spirit guides communicate with us all the time, but they do so with signs and symbols that speak to our subconscious minds where they can bypass the analytical, judgmental conscious mind that wants to ignore the signs, or explain them away as coincidence.

According to the website *Ask-Angels.com*, "The specific message depends on where you are in the present moment. It depends on what's happening in your life and how far you've progressed on your awakening path. At first, 11:11 could simply be a wake-up call from your Angels and from your higher self saying, 'Hey, we're here.' There's more going on than the physical dimension."

These time prompts allow us to focus in on what we are thinking and to bring us back into the present moment so we can ask whether our thoughts are serving us and directing us toward what we truly desire to manifest.

How often do we even think about the thoughts we are thinking? The vast majority of the time, we are *not* thinking about what we want, but instead of all the things that we don't like or need. Guess what? When we do that, we get more of them. But when we see 111 or 11:11, we can slow down and let our angels remind us to set our thoughts straight and even make sure we are sending the highest and best thoughts out into the collective.

Other numbers of the angels include:

222 – Newly planted ideas are taking root. Water and nurture them correctly and don't quit if you can't yet see the growth.
333 – Ascended Masters are nearby and ready to offer guidance and love if you call upon them. This can include Jesus, Mary, Moses, or any other spiritual master figure.
444 – You are surrounded by loving angels. *Do not worry!*
555 – Major life change ahead. *Buckle your seatbelt!*
666 – Your thoughts may be out of balance and more focused on the material. *Refocus* and get back to balance.
777 – You are doing great, and the angels are cheering on your progress.
888 – One cycle is about to end, and a new one will begin. Prepare and be ready to harvest the seeds you planted earlier.
999 – The end or completion of one phase in your life.
000 – You and God/Source are one.

Angel messages can also be a combination of different numbers. We can often feel the meaning behind these number sequences by using our intuition, which is our higher knowledge self within.

ACTIVATION DOORWAY

Another popular theory about the meaning of 11:11 comes from a spiritual author named Solara, who claims she had communications with interdimensional beings and learned about the Doorway of 11:11 into the Temple of Oneness. Her writings and teachings focus on 11:11 as a doorway to ascension. She believes the Activation of that doorway occurred on January 11, 1992. A Third Gate activation took place in 1997. The doorway of 11:11 closed on December 31, 2011, and the time afterward is devoted to individual transformation and freeing ourselves from duality's grip. She also believed that after the final closing of the doorway, there would be such a newness to everything it would be beyond worlds.

Needless to say, this didn't happen in visible and obvious ways, but for many of her followers, hopefully that newness and transformation happened so that one day soon we might reach a critical mass of enlightened souls.

For the many who call themselves "lightworkers," 11:11 is a symbolic number of great shift and transformation into a Golden Age that we are either in right now, or that will begin soon (there is some confusion as to when, much like the many dates ascribed to the Age of Aquarius).

GEORGE BARNARD AND URANTIA

Another popular figure in the 11:11 transformation movement is George Barnard of the 11:11 Progress Group. Barnard is a known figure in the lightworker world for his extensive work with what he calls "Midwayers," celestial beings that make up the Progress Group. The Midwayers were first introduced in *The Urantia Book* in 1955, a 2,055-page book that claims to be a divine revelation for Planet Earth. The book includes descriptions of higher dimensional beings, loving beings of the spirit called Midwayers, who interact with humans to assist us as we navigate the troubles of the world.

The Urantia Book, which serves as the basis for Barnard's work, has sold over a million copies and has been translated into fourteen languages. It even claims to include an authentic "celestial record" of the life of Jesus and his teachings (part 4 of the book).

The relationship to 11:11 comes from the intermingling of humans with celestial beings that we might even call "angels," for they can do things like stop us from dying in a car crash or prevent a deadly accident from taking place. Guardian angels, perhaps. *The Urantia Book* claims that these entities are "midway between mortals of the realms and the angelic orders; hence they are called midway creatures." According to the book, when digital clocks came into fashion, the Midwayers petitioned to claim 11:11 as their prompt to contact humans! Thus, seeing 11:11 meant that a Midwayer was trying to alert you to something, offer guidance, or get your attention.

Barnard had extensive contact with these Midwayers and teaches and lectures on what they are and what their messages are for humanity, focusing on the meanings of 11:11. The channeled messages the Progress Group receives, which are read by people all over the world, are intended to assist people who feel they may have a role to play in the transformation movement. The Progress Group helps them identify those roles and decipher the messages of the celestials that come in the form of number sequences.

THE SUBCONSCIOUS

Some might ask why our guides and angels don't just speak to us in our own language, so we cannot miss or mistake their guidance. Perhaps it has something to do with the real power player in our lives, the subconscious mind, which is responsible for approximately ninety percent of our behaviors, beliefs, and patterns. The subconscious does not respond to words as much as it does to symbols and patterns, because that is the language it operates on. Symbolic images, even when they appear as number sequences, speak to the deeper aspects of the mind and bypass the analytical chatter of the conscious mind. Time prompts and sequences like 11:11 may be understood by our subconscious, without ever being understood by our conscious mind, and that is by design, because the subconscious is where the most fundamental possibilities for change and awakening happen.

Remember, too, that signs and symbols can have different meanings to different people, according to their cultural and societal beliefs and upbringings. Yet we have found that 11:11 often means the very same thing to people of all walks of life—pay attention, wake up, rise up, ascend, be aware. So that suggests there is some deeper meaning at play that goes beyond the personal perspective, into the wild and wooly world of the "collective."

ARCHETYPES

But is there a deeper meaning behind these numbers, one that speaks to each of us on a collective, universal level? "The sequence of natural numbers turns out to be unexpectedly more than just a mere stringing together of identical units: it contains the whole of mathematics and everything yet to be discovered in the field."

Those are the words of Carl Jung. Most of us have been introduced to the work of Carl Jung and his concepts of archetypes and the collective unconscious, but just in case you were absent that week in school, here's a refresher.

Carl Gustav Jung was born in 1875 and was instrumental in the origins of the fields of psychotherapy and psychiatry. He was a student of the great Sigmund Freud, until the two parted ways over differences of opinions on some key theories related to sexuality, the subconscious, and dreams. But Jung went on to build a massive body of work involving the conscious, subconscious, and the "collective unconscious" levels of the mind.

We know about our conscious minds. That is the mind that sees and experiences and analyzes and processes the information our five senses are exposed to. The subconscious is the deeper part of the mind that, like the base of an iceberg, lies below the visible realm but is the powerhouse of creating our patterns of thought, behavior, and action. If you want to stop a bad habit or create a new life, you must know how to change the programming of the subconscious, or you will simply repeat the pattern and end up with what you always had.

The deepest part of the mind is the collective unconscious, which Jung believed was the realm of connectivity to the rest of the universe and to other living things. This realm is like a giant warehouse full of symbols and archetypes that are universal in nature and therefore understood by all humans regardless of age, color, creed, or background.

Archetypes are the "words" of the collective unconscious— symbols that are the original models from which all similar items of the same kind are created. They are the molds or blueprints of concepts and ideas that are understood by anyone and everyone because they speak to a common experience of being human. Before humans could write or even verbalize their ideas very well, we took to drawing simple figures and symbols on cave walls and rocks to convey information to others. Some of those symbols would be altered to take on meaning according to country of origin, religious beliefs, and traditions, but many stayed the same because they spoke to such a deep, common element of existence. They were, and are, unchangeable.

Archetypes can include everything from the "hero" and "villain" to the "leader," "teacher," "savior," and "demon." Again, concepts that can be understood by all because of their universality. And yes, numbers are archetypal as well. We have core meanings we assign to numbers just as we do to objects like birds, butterflies, and rockets.

Jung struggled with mathematics as a student and it was his later study of archetypes that gave him a new appreciation for those pesky numbers that had given him so much trouble. Many of his patients had dreams involving numbers, and Jung began to see how they were related to patterns and character traits the patients had that were being personified in their dreams in the form of a number or numeric sequence. Jung believed that small integers may be the oldest of archetypes involving order, because primitive humans would have used them to keep track of objects of importance and to measure things.

He also believed that smaller natural numbers corresponded with different levels of the human psyche. The number 1 would be the stage of non-differentiation. Two stood for polarity of opposites and opposition. Three represented a movement toward a resolution and was akin to the trinity. Four was the number of stability and wholeness. Thus, he linked numbers with traits and characteristics in much the same way numerologists do. Numbers took on an archetypal/universal quality that could be shared by all, because all human psyches go through the same model of evolution and development.

The archetype of order that numbers represent is probably the most important reason why so many people see, and resonate with, 11:11. Archetypes have incredible influence on and power over our subconscious minds, and therefore, our conscious behaviors, beliefs, and patterns, even if we are not aware of it. Because Jung believed that number was irreducible, he felt it was the most critical driver of bringing order out of chaos, and as an extension of that, the development of the field of mathematics paralleled the development of the human psyche.

Pythagoras was right when he said, "All is number," but even he may not have realized just how deep a statement that was! However, Jung and others who followed in his footsteps felt that the archetype label can really only be given to smaller numbers, because as we develop a need for bigger and bigger number sequences, it literally becomes impossible to ascribe any particular meaning to them other than a quantity. The smaller integers are where the magic is, allowing for the same primordial images of other archetypal images. Not only that, but the smaller integers are the basis for any larger number or numeric order, so that in and of itself makes them archetypal in the study of mathematics.

All of this played into the work Jung did connecting the physical world to the spiritual or inner world, unifying matter and the psyche, and noting the powerful links between physics and mathematics as well as the inner realms and workings of the human mind. According to mathematical principles, simple ideas and structures evolve into more complex ones. Jung believed that the same principal held true for the world of the mind via simple archetypes that evolve into the complex psyches and personalities that make us who we are.

THE DOORWAY TO SATAN?

The overwhelming majority of people experiencing 11:11 and other time prompts speak of positive, even empowering experiences. But to some, the time prompt is the doorway to the dark side. Synthia Esther, who founded Synthia Esther Ministries, claims that 11:11 is a doorway to Satan's world of the occult and warns that lightworkers, New Agers, Midwayers, angels, and guides, or anything metaphysical is a form of mass deception because of this belief, which is documented on her website, *www.sacredpursuit.org*.

The idea here is that 11:11 is part of the ongoing battle between God and Satan and that 11:11 is a calling card into the world of demons. This certainly presents a stark contrast to the metaphysical belief that it indicates positive, loving, joyful ascension and transformation. For those of a religious nature, the site uses biblical quotes to show that people who believe in godless myths will be punished and that they should even reject the Oneness movement, which teaches that there is just one God. Some also believe that fallen angels may be manipulating and recruiting people into believing the evil workings of the 11:11 movement and that any and all teachings of a spiritual, higher nature are a form of deceptive demonic control.

Perhaps it is up to each individual to decide whether seeing a number sequence over and over is a positive thing or a negative thing. The vast majority of people feel it is a positive force for individual and collective change and a way to lift the world to higher ground . . . but don't say we didn't warn you!

Chapter 2:2

THIS IS YOUR BRAIN ON NUMBERS

You don't have to be a mathematician to have a feel for numbers. —John Forbes Nash, Jr.

Remember the movie *Rain Man*? Dustin Hoffman played a man named Ray who had savant abilities when it came to numbers and mathematics. His brain could process information extremely quickly. So quickly in fact that what would take him a second . . . would take the rest of us a day to figure out. He could determine the number of toothpicks dropped on the floor by a waitress just by looking at the mess. The rest of us might venture a guess, but we'd not be close unless we got on the floor and counted them one by one ourselves.

NUMBER SENSE

The skills Ray had were extreme, but the truth is, we all have a region of the brain that senses quantities, and does so rather quickly. Just above each ear, there is a small patch of neurons responsible for giving us a sort of extrasensory perception of amounts and quantities. Some scientists even refer to it as a "number sense," much like our other five senses. According to an article on *npr.org* called "Scientists Put a Sixth Sense for Numbers on Brain Map," by Michaeleen Doucleff, these small groups of neurons located on either side of our brains help us to identify how many of an object we are seeing visually. Using functional magnetic resonance imaging, a team of scientists at Utrecht University in the Netherlands, led by Ben Harvey, showed subjects a series of circles from one to eight in number on a screen, then mapped their brain activity.

They saw a group of approximately 80,000 neurons (the size of a postage stamp) light up in the brains of all the subjects as they counted the circles. Interestingly, they determined that one side of the brain was more lit up when the subjects identified smaller numbers, and the other side lit up when exposed to larger numbers. It's as if we have two built-in brain calculators that identify a quantity, then adjust themselves to use more neurons to sense the higher quantity accordingly. The example they give is being able to quickly count five toothpicks but needing more time to quantify five hundred.

The brain also appears to map a "mental number line," according to the Scientific American article "Our Brains Have a Map for Numbers." Neuroscientists located a small brain area devoted to numerosity that operates along a continuous mapped region of the brain, similar to how we organize numbers from the lowest at the left to the highest at the right. Researchers in the Netherlands published a paper in the journal *Science* showing that a region in the right superior parietal lobe of the brain, which is in the upper back area, appears to map out the numerosity when the brain is exposed to a number of dots on a screen. On the edge of this patch, closer to the middle of the brain, small quantities are mapped. On the outside opposite edge of the brain, larger quantities. They literally identified a consistent map of subjects' brains that followed activity along the map to identify how many dots were seen—from smaller to bigger.

The parietal cortex area responded more to relative values and quantities, rather than absolutes, showing that different areas of the brain are responsible for processing quantities in a way that is relative to the experience. Areas of the brain associated with language were also involved, allowing us to make judgments of the numbers we are seeing. "Whether you're a math whiz or failed high school algebra, you can still readily judge, almost subconsciously, that there are about twenty books on a shelf or a few dogs running in the park," the article's author Emilie Reas, a neuroscience doctoral student at UC San Diego, states. Because infants and animals show this same skill, it may be an innate skill as much as hearing, sight, and touch.

Dr. Joseph Parvizi, an associate professor of neurology at Stanford, also conducted a study involving seven people with epilepsy. In the course of mapping activity in their brains, Parvizi discovered the same general area of the brain responsible for number and quantity processing—the inferior temporal gyrus that extends to both sides of the brain near the ear canals. Made of between one and two million cells, this neural network responds strongly to actual numbers and numeric quantities, yet it's close to the area of the brain that processes language and symbol interpretation. This allows people to read numbers and words together, and understand one, the other, and both without the brain overheating!

SEVEN DIGITS

On average, the longest chain of numbers a person can remember contains seven digits. Think of a telephone number for example. In the 1950s, psychologists labeled seven the magical number for the brain's active or working memory. In a study published in the journal *Physical Review Letters,* a neuroscientist at UC San Diego named Mikhail Rabinovich teamed with Christian Bick, a graduate student at the Max Planck Institute for Dynamics and Self-Organization in Gottingen, Germany, to show an actual picture of just how our brain neurons fire when we are asked to recall a number sequence, word sequence, or a sequence of steps such as driving instructions.

A cluster of neurons literally focus in on a word, number, or sequence one at a time, so that when we hear or see a series or sequence of words, numbers, or say driving directions, we can clearly follow and understand them, rather than have them all identified in a jumble that makes no sense or puts them out of order. Seven numbers or words seems to be the sweet spot where our brains are able to recall the information on the fly, with anything over that presenting greater and greater difficulty both in terms of actually remembering the words or numbers . . . and recalling the exact order they were first presented in.

Perhaps many of you have already experienced this when at the grocery store trying to remember the eight things you had on your grocery list (the one you left at home) and can only remember seven! It's not that our brains cannot handle more words and numbers. Obviously, we all have memorized things for school events, or dialog from a movie, that go well beyond the lucky seven limit. But for the most part, we can recall it a whole lot easier when we only have seven to recall. This can also explain why many people have such difficulty memorizing the lyrics of songs beyond the first couple of lines or remembering the middle and endings of famous poems.

The old parlor game "Telephone Operator" speaks to this as well. To play the game, people stand in a line and pass a piece of information to the next person and the person at the end then repeats what they were told. Most likely, it won't come close to what the first person actually said, because as you go down the line, people remember according to the individual capacity of their own brains and pass on what they think they heard. By the end, you've got a completely different sequence or phrase than you started with.

Savants may be able to use their brain's numeric power much more efficiently than the rest of humanity, but we all have the ability. We just need to know our personal limits. It appears our own brains are as primed and geared toward identifying numbers and numeric patterns as much as our conscious minds, but perhaps in smaller quantities. Yet for those who experience number sequences, time prompts, and synchronicities with numbers, and feel there is much more to it than simple brain function, the brain fails to do what only the mind can do . . . give these experiences meaning, even imply a deeper connection to something both internal and external that speaks a universal language meant to be identified by the brain and understood by the mind.

THE RAS

So, might there be a reason why our brains notice 11:11 and other time prompts that bridges the gap between the metaphysical and the physical, the world of spirit and the world of our brains? Yes, there is, and it is called the RAS—the Reticular Activating System. Although some choose to call it the "human GPS."

The RAS is a loose network of neural fibers and neurons that are clustered at the brain stem. Neurons in the RAS connect with other parts of the brain via two parts: the ascending RAS, and the descending RAS. The ascending RAS connects to the cortex, thalamus, and hypothalamus. The descending RAS connects to the cerebellum and all nerves responsible for our five senses.

The RAS has a role in sleep and wakefulness, eating, sex, walking, elimination, breathing, heartbeat, and even behavior and motivation, but what makes it so fascinating in terms of the time prompts that people report is the *way* it works. For such a small cluster, its functions are many, including giving our brains the ability to control what we consciously perceive, and thus what becomes a part of our reality.

So the RAS is a filter that literally sifts through hundreds of millions of bits of information coming at the brain every moment of every hour of every day, to help us focus on just the few bits that we need to for our daily survival. Out of approximately 400 million bits of information bombarding the brain, that can be as little as just forty bits. The rest is deemed unimportant and therefore does not become a part of our conscious awareness... until it does.

Let's say you see 11:11 once. Big deal. Then you see it again, and maybe a third time in a very short timeframe. Now your brain's RAS is alerted to zero in, like a GPS, on more 11:11s, because it has suddenly caught your attention and become important to you. All other stimuli coming at the brain, including sensory information like sights and sounds and smells, gets kicked to the rear, because your focus is now on seeing more of these time prompts as you marvel at the coincidence of it all and wonder what meaning it might have. You've made it more important than the other 399,999,960 bits of information coming at you, and now, you will see it everywhere.

Remember buying a car or a piece of clothing that you were certain was unique? Immediately after leaving the shop or dealership you began seeing it everywhere. Why had you not noticed it before? Because it wasn't important to you then, only now it is, and your RAS is now on full alert to see it everywhere you go. The RAS even works in your dreams, which is why some symbols and themes repeat themselves, as they are important to your subconscious mind, which speaks and understands the language of dreams. Psychotropic drugs have a strong effect on the RAS, too, which may explain the often-archetypal visions and images people see under their influence, images that under normal circumstances mean nothing but are extremely critical to the collective unconscious mind.

For the RAS, seeing 11:11 repeatedly becomes a top shelf focus for the brain, and when coupled with personal or collective meaning, it will continue to show up throughout your lifetime, until it becomes nonimportant or, as some believe, teaches you the lesson it is meant to teach you. In terms of the law of attraction teachings, what you focus on expands, and where your thoughts go, your reality manifests. The RAS assists with making sure that your actions and behaviors line up with the focus of your mind. If you are focused on poverty or anger, you tend to attract more poverty and reasons to be angry. If your focus is on being happy no matter what, you attract more happiness. No matter what. As simple as it sounds, it is more complex, but again, it's all about the brain actually determining what it will perceive and process based upon what is important or prominent in your thoughts.

Next time you see 11:11 or any other time prompt over and over, remember that even though your brain is doing what it does, there still may be a higher and more spiritual reason why those numbers are important to you and not others. That may be something only your subconscious, or collective unconscious, understands, but worry not, for those powerful parts of the mind drive your basic actions, beliefs, and behaviors. Ultimately, though, it's up to you to choose to wisely program, or reprogram, what goes into this vast database of information that has triggered your RAS into action from the time you were born.

Although there might be a sound scientific explanation for seeing time prompts and sequences (or even word sequences and symbols, for that matter), that doesn't automatically imply that they have no deeper meaning. Nor does it mean that they do. One thing we can say for sure is that people having these experiences know that something other than a neuron response or a change in focus is happening to them, and that it involves an actual shift in consciousness that opens them up to synchronistic and serendipitous experiences they would have otherwise missed.

An example of this would be someone seeing 4545 everywhere. They may be able to identify how it began with one situation where they needed to find a house with that number. That event made 4545 stand out as important amidst a sea of numbers because they needed to find that house. Over time, their RAS is still seeing 4545 because it is conditioned to see it, since it was important at one time. The pattern has been set, and the neural pathway has been created. Now, not seeing it becomes a more difficult challenge!

Now imagine that during a 4545 sighting, right at that time of focus and present moment awareness, something significant happens. Say you get a great solution to a long-term problem. You find the perfect ending to your novel. You hear the final notes of the song you've been writing. You avoid being hit by a car. The importance of that sequence becomes so ingrained in your brain, in the latter case as a survival mechanism, you then see it everywhere for the rest of your life and recall how it was critical to what you were dealing with at the time. Like a snowball rolling downhill, you now experience even more aha moments and wake-up pokes when you see 4545. Congratulations, this has become your own personal power prompt!

This is a great example of the brain and mind (or mind/consciousness) working in tandem to make sure that you get the information you need when you need it, in the language that is understood by the subconscious and collected unconscious . . . even if it isn't understood by the conscious mind right at the moment it happens.

As scientists continue to learn more about how the brain functions, and how consciousness works with the activity of the brain to create reality and perception, we will no doubt discover that what seems to be purely scientific and mundane is actually a part

> Look at the back of a $100 dollar bill; you may never have noticed it before, but if you count the windows on the smaller buildings (not including doors) to the right and left of the main part of Independence Hall, it adds up to 11 and 11. Is this part of some grand conspiracy to ingrain this mysterious number in our brains? A message from some secret society? Or could it just be coincidence?

Coincidence or not, the windows on either side add up to 11, a most mysterious number that seems to hold some meaning for many people. Image courtesy of U.S. Federal Reserve.

of a much larger process that allows us to have experiences that are both normal and "para"-normal, including liminal experiences where we sense that there is more to our world than meets the eye, nose, ear, mouth, and skin. Numbers may be the doorway to that sixth sense that links science with spirit.

WHY AND HOW NUMBERS EVOLVED

From the dawn of time, humankind realized that it needed a way to measure things, to count things, to understand the quantity of things. In the beginning, man had the need to simply track ownership. From this basic need, numbers were born and have been utilized in such a manner ever since. Later, the economics of trade and barter necessitated the need for more.

The first known use of numbers as objects for purposes of counting is said to date back to approximately 40,000 to 30,000 BC, according to scholar Georges Ifrah, author of *The Universal History of Numbers*, when bones and artifacts with distinct "tally marks" have been dated. Prehistoric humans may also have used their basic understanding of numbers to help them track the stars through the sky, divide day and night into time frames, keep tabs on flocks of birds and herds of animals, and even track the growth of their children. Eventually, the crudeness of tally marks upon bone and stone was replaced with far more complex representations, but Ifrah states that tally sticks, as crude as they might seem, were still in use until fairly recently by Native American labor workers.

Ifrah calls tally marks "one-for-one correspondence," which "allows the simplest of minds to compare two collections of beings or things, of the same kind or not, without calling on the ability to count in numbers." For millennia, primitive peoples used this one-for-one correspondence with the things they had available at the time, such as bone, rock, or sheep.

The first known written numbering system, according to Ifrah's book, came to us from the fourth millennium BC in Elam. It was here that the pebble-method of accounting was discovered and used by accountants using "molded, unbaked clay tokens in the place of ordinary or natural pebbles." Each token had a different value representing a unit of one or higher, and even tokens of different shapes represented a specific value, that is, a small pellet might be 10, and a larger rock might be 100.

It is the subject of debate among anthropologists, historians, and mathematicians as to whether disparate cultures developed their own number systems, or the ideas of using numbers was somehow "seeded" from a handful of more technologically advanced cultures, which then spread. Most agree that our own numeric system is based upon the Hindu-Arabic system. The majority of experts also agree that cardinal numbers (1,2,3 . . .) then led to ordinals (1st, 2nd, 3rd, and so on), and may have been the result of using fingers and digits to place objects in a specific order. And you always thought it was a joke about using both hands and feet to count!

Other than the typical crude bone and stone tally markers of our cave-dwelling ancestors, the development of numbers seems to have closely paralleled the development of culture, language, and higher knowledge. The oldest of cultures represented numbers with the repeated use of pictorial images to represent a particular object. Nowhere was this more obvious than in the Egyptian culture, which employed three types of number systems: the hieroglyphic, the hieratic, and the demotic.

Egyptian Numbering Systems

The hieroglyphic is the most widely recognized system, and was often written on stone. Hieroglyphics were not specifically focused on "numbers," as it was a much more formal mode of language. The hieratic, or temple writing, was more commonly used by priests, and was written on papyrus. The demotic system emerged from the hieratic and became the commonplace system of textual writing. Egyptian numbers were written right to left and the numbers 1 through 9 were represented by vertical lines or strokes. Higher numbers were represented by more symbolic shapes, such as the coil of rope for 100, and the man with upraised arms for 1,000,000 (this makes sense, for who would *not* raise up their arms upon receipt of 1,000,000 objects!).

Sumerian Numbers

The ancient Sumerians and Babylonians adopted the use of symbols to represent numeric groupings. The Sumerians, using the base-60, or sexagesimal system, actually only had two numbers to deal with, 1 and 10, and all other digits combined the two symbols accordingly. Early Babylonians, using both the base-10 and base-60 systems, developed a series of vertical strokes and triangular shapes to indicate both low and high numbers. Amounts were represented by a corresponding increase or decrease in the number of lines and triangles. Interestingly enough, these simple systems rarely included the concept of zero.

Mayan Numbers

Other cultures, such as the Maya, used various types of horizontal strokes and dots to represent number groupings. Both the Maya and Aztecs operated on the vigesimal system of base-20, which is unlike the denary (base-10) system that is in use today. Their numbers combined sticks, bars, and dots, and unlike previous numeric systems, even included a shell-like symbol to represent the concept of "zero."

Chinese Numbers

The Chinese system shares some common patterns with current Chinese numbers, and utilized a "rod system" and was derived from the ancient use of sticks of wood on counting boards. The concept of zero was indicated by a square, and higher numbers were written in monogram form. Vertical lines were added to the tops and bottoms of the sticks to represent increased numeric values. Also known as "math sticks," this ancient method of counting has been traced back seven thousand years to the Yangshao culture, according to an article

This Is Your Brain on Numbers

The Maya used lines and dots to create their number system. Image courtesy of Wikipedia.

in the *UNESCO Courier* by Du Shi-ran, titled "The Math Sticks of Early China—Chinese Calculation Using Counting Rods."

Earthenware shards excavated in the Henan and Shanxi Chinese Provinces show inscribed marks that are a combination of vertical lines. This early arrangement is believed to be the most ancient numeric system to have emerged from China. Early Chinese mathematicians used counting rods, which were sticks made of bamboo called "chou." These sticks were arranged into configurations, which were used to perform calculations. This became known as "chou suan," or "calculating with chou."

A more modern Chinese numeric system involved the use of "oracle bones" by the Shang people, upon which some five thousand Chinese characters were inscribed as a way of tracking the number of birds and animals that were both hunted and sacrificed. These systems evolved throughout the millennia, and eventually became the present-day Chinese characters.

Aztecs

According to new research by mathematician Maria del Carmen Jorge y Jorge of the National Autonomous University of Mexico, the Aztecs, on the other side of the world, also used combinations of hearts, arrows, hands, bones, and arms in their system of measurement. Working with geographer Barbara Williams, del Carmen Jorge y Jorge examined the Codex Vergara, an ancient Aztec land-surveying book, and discovered unequivocal correlations between land plot lengths and the combinations of images. The researchers also found a very surprising correlation: 60 percent of the fields matched the basic surveying calculations used today, and many of the fields were sloped and terraced, indicating a remarkable understanding of agricultural methodology.

The Aztec's agricultural and engineering successes prove that even this type of crude measurement provided an acceptable level of accuracy.

The ancient Romans, Greeks, and Hebrews used alphabetic systems that included a letter of their alphabet corresponding to a number. The 22 letters of the Hebrew alphabet represent the numbers 1 to 400, with numbers above that represented by composition. For example, the number 500 would be represented by the corresponding letters for 400 and 100.

Roman Numerals

Similarly, the Greeks and Romans also used an alphabetic number system. The Greeks actually had two systems. Their first system, which was in place through the 1st century BC, used initial letters that corresponded to each number, again combining them with the letter for the digit 5 to create larger numbers. Dots indicated numbers in the hundreds, and a bar was placed to the left of the numbers to indicate thousands. The Greek system, known as "Isopsephy" (which roughly translates to "equal pebble"), referred to the earlier practice of using pebbles to create patterns for learning basic math and geometrics. This early method is related to the Hebrew Gematria and has links to Masonic number symbolism, which is in use today.

Roman numerals may have been based upon the number 5, used specific letters to indicate the digits 1, 5, 10, 50, 100, 500, and 1,000. For some numbers, instead of "adding on" to existing number/letters, the Romans chose to do things a little bit differently by incorporating the "subtractive principle." An example would be the number 9, which is 10, or X, preceded by a 1, or I, resulting in IX, rather than VIIII, a 5 with four 1s after it.

Current Times

Today, we use a hybrid number system referred to as the Indian-Arabic. It is one of three main families of symbol sets that utilize the Hindu-Arabic Numeral System. According to Wikipedia, this system is defined as a "positional decimal system," and dates back to the 9th century. This arrangement is designed "for positional notation in a decimal system," using decimal points to indicate the separation of placement of 1s from the 10ths place. There are only two other families using this positional numeral system: the eastern Arabic numerals used in Egypt, and the Indian numerals used in India.

Our well-loved digits 0 through 9 were initially developed in India from earlier Brahmi numerals, between the 2nd century BC and the 6th century AD. Although we generally refer to this system as Arabic (because it was the Arabs who taught these numbers to the Europeans in the Middle Ages) some historians suggest that the numbers 0 through 9 were actually first used in parts of West Asia. Their hypothesis is that this system quickly spread into Europe in the 10th century AD via the work of Arabic astronomers and mathematicians. The very first inscription found to use the number 0 came from the western Arabic world as well, around 870 AD, but Indian documents on copper plates also show the use of 0 as far back as the 1st century AD.

Once the exclusive purview of mathematicians, the Indian-Arabic system is now the most widely used and recognized in the world. Two mathematicians, the Persian Al-Khwarizmi and his Arabic colleague Al-Kindi, are credited with the spread of the Indian-Arabic system throughout the Middle East and into the West via their books *On the Calculation with Hindu Numerals* and *On the Use of the Indian Numerals*, respectively. Both tomes, written between 825 and 830 AD, were the later foundation for 10th-century Middle Eastern mathematicians who expanded the original system to include fractions.

Base Systems

Starting with base systems, we find that there is indeed a way to measure everything, from the amount of information a computer can process to how many yak can cross a ravine in three weeks.

Digital computers use the binary, or base-2, system in general, to represent two states of transistor voltage, either high or low, one or zero. The binary system is often equated with states of "on" or "off." In comparison, many ancient cultures utilized the base-5 system (quinary), most likely because that is how many fingers they had on each hand! But the Yuki, a Native American tribe in Northern California, took that idea one step further, developing a base-8 system that included the spaces between fingers, yet only included digits up to 8. This novel idea is certainly unique among the various system permutations.

By far, the most popular system in the world is the base-10 decimal system. Widely used today, its origin is also allegedly linked to the total number of human fingers. Yes, the next obvious system would be base-20, as we have twenty fingers and toes combined, and many Pre-Columbian Mesoamerican cultures, such as the Maya, used this vigesimal system.

Another system, the base-12, also gained popularity. The duodecimal and dozenal base-12 systems are used in multiplication and division, and led to the popularity of the "dozen" quantitative measurement. Also, 12 is a common unit of measurement in the United States. There are 12 inches in a foot, and day and night are divided into 12-hour chunks of time. On a more epicurean note, not only was the famous "Philly Cheese Steak" originally created as a 12-inch delicacy but also most pizza joints' standard size pie is 12 inches.

The base-60, or sexagesimal, system is also a familiar one as it is used in our measurement of time. As we all know, there are 60 seconds in a minute, and 60 minutes in an hour. This system was used by many Mesopotamian cultures, including the Sumerians, and may have originated by combining the base-10 and base-12 systems. Proof of this is demonstrated in the Chinese calendar, which uses a base-60 system to denote years, yet gives two "symbols" to each year, one base-10 and one base-12 (the base-12 corresponding with the twelve animals of the Chinese Zodiac).

Just as a variety of base systems were developed to fit specific needs, mathematicians also developed varying types of numbers. Fortunately, for the average person, the "real" basic digits (1 to 10), as well as a modicum of addition, subtraction, multiplication, and division skills will suffice for the vast majority of everyday needs.

But for those truly obsessed with the magnetic power of numeric possibility, or those in scientific and other fields that actually require more than just the basics, settling just for the real digits, would be, well, unreal.

Zero

What we know about the origin of zero is that it seems to have appeared in various cultures around the same time.

The word *zero* comes from the Italian *zefiro* via the Arabic *afira*, meaning "it was empty" or "nothing." This was used originally in the translation of the Sanskrit *nya*, meaning "void" or "empty" (think also "null"). In the second millennium BC, the Babylonians were indicating a positional value for zero in their numeral system. Indian scholars such as Pingala were using the Sanskrit word for zero (*nya*) as far back as the 2nd century BC.

Even the ancient Greeks waxed poetic about the existence of zero. In fact, it became a topic of philosophical discussion, and religious scholars joined the debate during the medieval period. Scholars questioned the concept of "nil." How could there be such a thing as nothing? Yet already, most numeric systems were indeed making a special place for zero, either as a true number used alone, or, as a placeholder to create a specific context. Once the Hindu decimal system we use today spread from western Arabia into Europe, the concept of zero or nil spread along with it.

A true zero was also utilized in the Roman numeral system, sometime around 523 AD, with the word *nulla* meaning "nothing" and leading to the widespread use of the word by most medieval mathematicians. Another very early documented use of true zero dates back to 628 AD in the *Brahmasphutasiddhanta*, later spreading into China and the Middle Eastern Islamic world. But in 1229 AD, the Roman Catholic Church banned the use of zero, stating it was a Godless number because division by zero resulted in infinity.

Thankfully, a medieval monk and abacus counter named Raoul de Laon reintroduced the concept of zero into western Europe, despite pressure from Italian bankers and abacus users who objected to the "empty" number on their books! Zero soon became a sort of underground symbol used by merchants and smugglers who used the number in their "account keeping."

Infinity

At the other end of the spectrum, the idea of a never-ending number, or "infinity," had its earliest recorded mention in the *Isha Upanishad* of the Indian *YajurVeda* circa the 3rd century BC. The reference, "If you remove a part from infinity or add a part to infinity, still what remains is infinity" is the first known written idea of the infinite. The Indian mathematical text *Surya Prajnapti* categorized numbers into three sets: enumerable, innumerable, and the infinite. This set system was quite complex for its time and was later adapted by the Jain sect, who believed that even infinity had various subdivisions: infinite in length, infinite in volume, infinite in area, and perpetual infinity (dimensional). The mind boggles at the infinite possibilities.

The symbol which is commonly associated with infinity may have its origins rooted in the Latin *lemniscus,* meaning "ribbon." Anthropologists and historians suggest that this symbol may have originated with the Tibetan rock carvings of the ouroboros, or "world snake," which is also associated with infinity and a never-ending circle.

The one person who has been most readily associated with the origin of the infinity symbol is John Wallis (1616–1703). Wallis was an English mathematician who is also partially credited with the creation of calculus. As a tribute to his important contributions, Wallis also has an asteroid named after him called *Asteroid 31982 Johnwallis.*

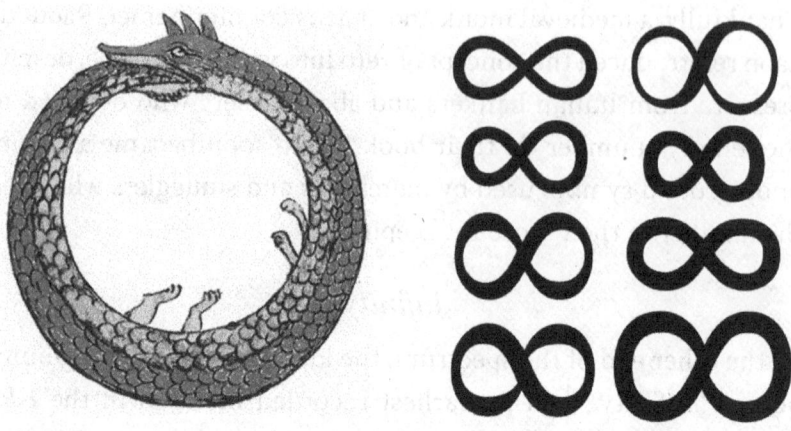

From nothing to everything, numbers run the gamut. In between these two extremes, the following have emerged:

- Natural Numbers—The integers we use every day, from zero to 1, 2, 3, 4, and onward. These are our counting numbers, therefore, our natural numbers, represented by N.
- Negative Numbers—Integers less than zero, opposites of positive numbers (anything over a zero!), and are usually written using a "minus" symbol, as in –7. Therefore, the opposite of 7 is –7. We use the Z to indicate negative integers.
- Real Numbers—All measuring numbers, usually written using decimal points to indicate position.
- Rational Numbers—Numbers that can be expressed as a fraction, with the numerator (which is the top of the fraction, for the mathematically challenged!), a natural integer, and the denominator (bottom of fraction), a natural number other than zero. All rational numbers are also considered real numbers (which means that it can be written in decimal form as well as fraction form). Confused yet?

- Irrational Numbers—Opposite of rational numbers. Pi is also an irrational number that we will look at in a later chapter. Irrational numbers are not crazy, they are just not rational.
- Complex Numbers—A set of numbers that are represented as C and allow a negative number to have a square root. The origin of complex numbers dates back to Heron of Alexandria in the 1st century AD. Complex numbers occur when you put a real number and an imaginary number together. Don't attempt this at home without adult supervision.
- Computable Numbers—Also known as recursive numbers or "computable reals," these are real numbers that can be "computed to within any desired precision by a finite, terminating algorithm." Suffice to say, you don't need to know these to balance your checkbook.
- Palindromic Numbers—Palindromes are numbers with digits that read the same backward as forward. 23432 is a palindromic number. They are used in recreational mathematics where palindromic numbers with special properties are sought. A "palindromic prime" is a palindromic prime number.
- Superreal Numbers—Take real numbers and extend them by adding either infinitesimally small numbers or infinitely large numbers. Why do this? Only a mathematician knows for sure.
- Imaginary Numbers—Numbers we give the special letter I symbol to in an example to represent an unknown or imagined property. They can also be defined as "a number whose square is a negative real number." Still following us?
- Prime Numbers—A prime number (or a prime) is "a natural number greater than 1, which has exactly two distinct natural number divisors: 1 and itself." An infinitude of prime numbers exists, as demonstrated by Euclid around 300 BC. The first

thirty prime numbers are: 2, 3, 5, 7, 11, 13, 17, 19, 23, 29, 31, 37, 41, 43, 47, 53, 59, 61, 67, 71, 73, 79, 83, 89, 97, 101, 103, 107, 109, and 113, according to Wikipedia. Prime numbers are a part of "number theory," the branch of mathematics that studies natural numbers.

- Mythical Numbers—Numbers that don't really exist except in the minds of man and myth. Mythical numbers are often accepted as fully factual, yet have no exact origin. Max Singer of the Hudson Institute coined the term in 1971. An example of this would be the popular claim that humans only use 10 to 12 percent of their brains. Most of us know the truth—they use far less! Another mythical number is 20—for the twenty times most grandmothers suggest you chew your food before swallowing (in order to aid digestion).
- Indefinitive/Fictitious Numbers—Numbers of a "ginormous" size used for comical effect or exaggeration. Examples would be: zillion, jillion, gazillion, and umpteen. These terms serve to take numbers far beyond the point of, say, hundreds of billions, but come just short of reaching infinity.

These all serve a distinct purpose for the many branches of mathematics developed to solve the problems of reality. Simple division. Algebra. Calculus. Geometry. Trigonometry. Were these constructs designed to torture and confuse us? Perhaps, but, more importantly, they all play significant roles in measuring and quantifying everything around us.

Chapter 3:3

SACRED SEQUENCES AND COSMIC CODES

Numbers are peculiar animals. They can unlock secrets, split atoms, reveal the inner workings of people and machines or draw patterns of outstanding complexity and beauty.
—Dame Anita Roddick, Numbers

When buildings talk, it is never with a single voice.
—Alain de Botton, The Architecture of Happiness

Throughout time immemorial, numeric sequences, patterns, and codes have proven useful to humans. As a significant part of our daily lives, they have also become an integral part of the mystery, mystique, and magic of the human experience. Many forms of music, cosmology, art, architecture, and nature incorporate patterns and sequences that, while appearing to be haphazard on the surface, under deeper examination reveal commonalities simply too deliberate to be random or accidental. Nowhere else is this more significant than in the mysterious and enigmatic world of sacred geometry.

Sacred geometry constitutes the foundation of the design of sacred architecture and art. Geometrical and mathematical ratios, harmonics, and proportion are found in music, light, cosmology, and natural structure, and these ratios have, at their respective foundations, a divine origin. Among the uses of sacred geometrical proportions are the building of structures such as temples, mosques, megaliths, monuments, and churches; the location and placement of sacred spaces such as altars, temenoi, and tabernacles; meeting places such as sacred groves, village greens, and holy wells; as well as the creation of religious art, iconography, and symbolism.

Again, the underlying premise behind sacred geometry is that there is a divine influence and connection between objects and their physical placement and measurements. It is believed by some that this divine influence can, if studied and dissected, lead to a transformative understanding of a greater reality at play in the universe.

Mathematician Heinrich Hertz is quoted as saying, "We cannot escape the feeling that these mathematical formulae have an independent existence and an intelligence of their own, that they are wiser than we are, wiser even than their discoveries, that we get more out of them than was originally put into them." For those who designed architecture, created art, and formed structures around the mystery of numbers, that intelligence came from a heavenly source.

PYTHAGORAS

We might say that the worship of numbers began with the famed Greek mathematician Pythagoras. Pythagoras lived from approximately 572 BC to 490 BC and was the founder of a monastic religious movement called, not surprisingly, Pythagoreanism. This group espoused the mysticism of math and philosophy. Pythagoras, known as "the father of numbers," is said to have made major contributions to many areas of study, yet few scholars can pinpoint definitive proof, suggesting that perhaps some of his greatest ideas and accomplishments may not have been his own!

Nevertheless, the followers of this man of wisdom (who called themselves "Pythagoreans") spent their days living under strict cultural rules of conduct, eating no meat and disowning all personal possessions. In many ways a school, the inner circle of this organization, called the "Mathematikoi," and the outer circle, the "Akousmatikoi," under Pythagoras's influence, studied religion and mathematics under the cloak of secrecy. Eventually, the inner and outer circles clashed and split off, leaving Pythagoras's own wife, Theano, in charge of those closest to the teacher himself.

In addition to his interest in math and the magic of numbers, Pythagoras was fascinated with music theory and harmonics. One of his most intriguing theories regards the "harmony of the spheres." His belief was that the movement of the planets and stars corresponded with mathematical equations as well as musical notes, thus producing a "symphony of the spheres."

Many of his other beliefs, such as reincarnation, the transmigration of souls, and life after death, heavily influenced other deep thinkers of his time. At one point, Pythagoras even went so far as to suggest that the very essence of being, or reality, is number, and that knowledge of one's own essence must come from a deeper understanding of number and the study of mathematics.

Plato

Pythagoras was a recognized influence upon another famous individual—the classical Greek philosopher Plato (428/427 BC to 348/347 BC). Plato, who was a student of Socrates and teacher of Aristotle, was one of the most critical forces behind the philosophical foundations of Western culture. Plato, also a mathematician, was founder of the Academy in Athens, which was believed to have been the first institution of higher learning in the Western world. Plato's own studies into music and harmonics suggest that he was influenced by a third-generation Pythagorean named Archytas, who contributed a great deal to geometry.

Mysterium Magnum

Some scholars have linked the ancient secretive society of Pythagoreans to more modern secret orders such as the Rosicrucians, Knights Templar, and Masons. These groups have rich histories rife with the teachings of sacred geometry and mystical mathematics. Often incorporating the concept of the "Mysterium Magnum" (Latin for "great mystery") and usually associated with alchemy and mysticism, they were (and continue to be) a cause for frequent speculation, rumor mongering, and scholarly debate.

The Mysterium Magnum, also called the "Great Design," denoted a universal source energy from which all of the Classical Elements emerged. This concept bears striking similarities to both the Zero Point Field of quantum physics as well as the Akashic Records of renowned clairvoyant and healer Edgar Cayce. Indeed, the patterns and proportions ascribed to geometrically inspired objects were thought to be inspired by heavenly forces, and by all accounts, would seem to suggest a Great Designer.

Golden Ratio

Not surprisingly, the natural world offers a plethora of examples of divine and intelligent patterns ripe for analysis. Many of these patterns are even present in the structure of living organisms! Two of the most stunning examples are the Golden Ratio and the Fibonacci spiral, both of which imply a higher order of measurement behind what many of us take for granted, such as our own bodies... or a seashell.

The Golden Ratio, also known as the Divine Ratio, the Golden Ration, and Golden Mean, is an irrational number of approximately 1.618033988749. One might ask why that specific ratio would be

Sacred Sequences and Cosmic Codes

The Golden Ratio, or Golden Mean.

any more "divine" than any other. Perhaps only the Great Designer knows for sure, but this ratio is found throughout the natural, scientific, and manmade worlds as the highest expression of balance, symmetry, and aesthetics. This fundamental formula can be described as "the ratio whereby the ratio of the whole to the larger section equals the ratio of the larger section to the smaller section."

Referred to as "phi," this ratio is present in many sacred icons such as the measurements of the Great Pyramid of Giza, the structure of a five-pointed star, a Pentagram (a sacred object to followers of Plato and Pythagoras), and even in the outline of the Acropolis near Athens, Greece (which takes the shape of a Golden Rectangle). Most notably, as represented by Leonardo da Vinci's famous Vitruvian Man, the Golden Ratio is present in the structure of the human body, with outstretched arms and legs showing the Golden Ratio at work.

da Vinci's Creations

The Vitruvian Man got its name from the ancient Roman architect, Vitruvius, whose "De Architectura" has been credited as being the inspiration for da Vinci's use of the Golden Ratio in his scientific and artistic endeavors. The drawing itself was found around 1487 AD as a part of da Vinci's many written journals that were filled with notes and diagrams of his intellectual and philosophical musings. Da Vinci was apparently so enamored of the Golden Ratio that

This derivation of the Vitruvian Man by Leonardo da Vinci depicts nine historical units of measurement: the yard, the span, the cubit, the Flemish ell, the English ell, the French ell, the fathom, the hand, and the foot. The Vitruvian Man was drawn to scale, so the units depicted are displayed with their proper histprical ratios. Image courtesy of Wikipedia Commons.

According to da Vinci's notes, the following ratios were present in the male human figure:

he included it in his famous *The Last Supper* painting. The overall composition of the painting contains three vertical Golden Rectangles, and one decagon (a Golden Ratio shape) in the figure of Jesus.

The Last Supper is a 15th-century mural painting da Vinci created for his patron Duke Ludovico Sforza and his duchess Beatrice d'Este. The painting measures 460 by 880 centimeters (15 feet by 29

- a palm is the width of four fingers.
- a foot is the width of four palms (that is, 12 inches).
- a cubit is the width of six palms.
- a man's height is four cubits (and thus 24 palms).
- a pace is four cubits.
- the length of a man's outspread arms is equal to his height.
- the distance from the hairline to the bottom of the chin is one-tenth of a man's height
- the distance from the top of the head to the bottom of the chin is one-eighth of a man's height.
- the maximum width of the shoulders is a quarter of a man's height.
- the distance from the elbow to the tip of the hand is one-fifth of a man's height.
- the distance from the elbow to the armpit is one-eighth of a man's height.
- the length of the hand is one-tenth of a man's height.
- the distance from the bottom of the chin to the nose is one-third of the length of the head.
- the distance from the hairline to the eyebrows is one-third of the length of the face.

Courtesy of Wikipedia.

feet) and is found in the back halls of the dining hall at Santa Maria delle Grazie in Milan, Italy. In addition to the Golden Rectangles and decagon, the painting makes references to the number 3, which most likely represents the Trinity, in the groupings of the Apostles, the number of windows behind Jesus, and Jesus' own triangular shape in the image.

The famous Last Supper mural depicts the Golden Ratio in art.

Da Vinci also used the Golden Rectangle for the face of his Mona Lisa, giving her the kind of profile that women today generally pay thousands of dollars to plastic surgeons for (maybe that's why she's smirking!). According to measurements, the Golden Ratio is present in the ratio of the width of her forehead compared to the length of the top of her head to her chin.

Impressionist painter George Seurat, creator of the drawing technique of pointillism, often used the Golden Section in his works, believing, as da Vinci did, that this heavenly ratio had an aesthetic value and beauty to which the human eye was naturally drawn. Other geometric ratios, although not necessarily designed for aesthetic value, can be found in Celtic and Indian art, as well as in the design of labyrinths and mandalas, where symmetry and measurement were intended to create a spiritual resonance between object and observer. Much to the joy of "circle watchers"—individuals who study the phenomenon of crop circles—there have been suggestions that they encompass similar types of geometric ratios.

FIBONACCI

One of the most important and well-known Golden Ratios comes from the discovery by an Italian with a whole lot of names. Leonardo of Pisa was born in 1170 AD and went by the names Leonardo Pisano, Leonardo Bonacci, Leonardo Fibonacci, and finally just Fibonacci. Could you imagine what his driver's license would look like today? His name comes from "filius Bonacci," or "son of Bonaccio," a nickname that was originally given to his father. No matter which name he goes by, Fibonacci is responsible for the spread of the Hindu-Arabic numeral system into Europe, as well as the number sequence now named after him.

In his 13th-century book, *Book of Calculation*, or *Liber Abaci*, this brilliant and creative mathematician used the knowledge he had gleaned regarding the mathematical systems used in the Middle Eastern countries during his travels throughout Northern Africa. With that knowledge, he went on to further the development of a previously discovered sequence of numbers (Indian mathematicians were using the sequence as early as the 6th century AD) that is now called the Fibonacci sequence—a series of numbers designed in such a manner that each number after the first two numbers is the sum of the previous two numbers:

0, 1, 1, 2, 3, 5, 8, 13, 21, 34, 55, 89, 144, and so on . . .

In *Liber Abaci*, Fibonacci used this sequence as an example of the growth rate of a hypothetical rabbit population by using a number that showed the generation-by-generation increase. Beyond rabbits, this sequence is also found throughout nature as an inherent structural pattern in which the higher the numbers in the sequence, the closer the two consecutive numbers divided by each other will approach the Golden Ratio of 1:1.618. In the natural world, we see the Fibonacci sequence at work in many instances, such as the branching rate of plants. In several distinct species of flora, not only do the branch levels follow the pattern but also the spacing of the leaves match the number sequence! Some of the flower species that follow this pattern are buttercups, delphiniums, sunflowers, asters, and lilies.

A great many examples of "floral sequencing" can be found online (search Flower Fibonacci Sequence). One representation involves the purple passionflower, or *passiflora incarnata*. On the back of this flower there are three "sepals," the nonpetal part of flower, that protect the bud and make up the outermost layer. This layer is then followed by five outer green petals. Finally, there is an inner layer of five more paler green petals. On the front of the flower there are five greenish T-shaped stamens in the center, followed by three "deep brown carpels and style branches."

Other examples of the Golden Ratio (or Golden Mean) in nature include the manner by which lightning branches out, the way a tree spans its branches for maximum sunlight exposure, the way rivers branch, and even the proportions of the bodies and wingspans of birds and flying insects. Snowflakes and crystals also show distinct geometric patterns of formation, as does the coded "language" of our DNA.

Nature definitely seems to have received more than its fair share of Fibonacci sequences. The Chambered Nautilus (*Nautilus pompilius*), which is a marine creature of the cephalopod family, grows at a rate that matches the Fibonacci sequence. This creature has the honor of being partly responsible for the naming of yet another Fibonacci permutation—the Fibonacci spiral. This spiral configuration allows the growth of the shelled creature to be accommodated in a logarithmic spiral, without changing its actual shape as it grows. Honeybees also construct hexagon-shaped cells to hold their honey stores, which have prompted many scientists to suggest that the Fibonacci patterns may actually be a logical outcome

The Fibonacci spiral and the pattern in block form. Images courtesy of Wikipedia.

of natural principles, rather than the mysterious "signature of the Gods" that many Sacred Geometrists have labeled them.

OTHER SEQUENCES

According to Pythagoras, it was numeric sequences such as this, or numbers that expressed ratios, that were of far greater importance than the simple singular units we most often use in our day-to-day lives. Pythagoreans looked at these mysterious sequences as proof that there was an underlying layer of reality beneath that which we experienced, and that it was powered by numbers and the connections between them.

Even when expanded to a more macrocosmic level, there appears to be ample evidence of sacred patterns at play. The belief that the cosmos contained a geometric underlying reality is not new, and persists today with modern science and cosmology. It is believed that Johannes Kepler, the German astronomer and mathematician, is responsible for promoting a worldview that combines the sacred with the geometric. Known best for his laws of planetary motion, Kepler, once an assistant to the brilliant astronomer Tycho Brahe, often combined his knowledge of astronomy and astrology while also incorporating aspects of religious, spiritual, and philosophical arguments into his studies. During Brahe's time, this was deeply frowned upon; however, it did not discourage his zeal. He truly believed that there was an intelligent and divinely created plan to the universe that could be accessed through reason. This theory, which he termed "celestial physics," may have been a supplemental line of study to Aristotle's earlier *Metaphysics* and *On the Heavens*.

KEPLER

Kepler, whose love of astronomy began early in childhood, was at one time a theology student and attended seminary, yet he had an intense interest in astrology. Although the two disciplines may seem to be in opposition, surprisingly, there are many similarities. Kepler was so skilled in astrology that he was often called upon by his fellow students to do readings for them. Due in part to the melding of his understanding of theological and astrological principles, Kepler later formulated his treatise of a divinely inspired geometrical reality to the universe. This theory later became known as the Kepler platonic solid model. Once the basic framework was established, the view took the form of a sectioned model that showed the layers of the universe in accordance with his Great Cosmic Mystery, or "Mysterium Cosmographicum." This idea deeply reflected his own excitement for the Copernican system and its potential to bridge both the physical and the spiritual realms. So certain was he of his beliefs, that he even published a more detailed follow-up to the "Mysterium" in 1621 to further elaborate upon his initial writing.

Kepler's belief system echoed the popular worldview of the time among those who believed that the nature of reality was geometrically structured. This worldview combined the complexities of the best scientific modalities of the time involving space, matter, and time with religious symbolism and metaphysical concepts thrown in for good measure. According to this, all of existence fit together in a pattern, akin to a giant cosmic jigsaw puzzle, and the creator of this puzzle was the Great Designer. The Great Designer was an omnipotent entity whose laws operated on a higher order, yet manifested in the simplest of things, such as the petals of a flower.

SACRED NUMBERS

In his book *Sacred Number and the Origins of Civilization*, author Richard Heath states that the four mathematical arts of arithmetic, geometry, musical harmony, and astronomy comprise the "Quadrivium." These four elements were considered essential elements in the building of megalithic monuments. The idea behind this, again, was that "the field of number provided the foundation for all these numerical sciences. From this foundation a full numerical worldview would have been possible—one that found its fullest expression within the design, location, and structure of ancient monuments." But before we venture into a discussion of sacred structures, we first need to look more closely at the finer intricacies involved in determining the sacred from the mundane.

Even the realm of music does not escape the inclusion of intricate, number-based patterns. Harmonics are, at their source, nothing more than simple mathematical sequences of sound, notes, and chords that create resonance. Once again, the relationship between geometry, mathematics, and music can be attributed to Pythagoras. It was he who, through experimentation, discovered that strings that were stopped at certain points along their length would produce certain notes or octaves, and that certain ratios produced intervals that, as Pythagoras believed, had certain powers of healing. Followers of Pythagoras believed that musical harmony produced physical and spiritual harmony. Physician Hans Jenny, while being somewhat skeptical of the healing powers of music, was a firm believer in the connection between geometric figures and wave interactions. Jenny's research in this field led to the development of cymatics, in which he elaborated upon ancient knowledge provided by Pythagoras and the ancient Egyptians.

In his book *The Spiritual Technology of Ancient Egypt*, noted author and researcher Edward Malkowski examines how the Pythagorean Science of Numbers developed to show the relationship between numbers and, as Aristotle claimed, "the first principles of all things." Malkowski concludes that "At the heart of Pythagoras' science of numbers was the belief that all relationships could be reduced to number associations, and that all things are in fact number." This science of number was discovered through the science, or art, of music. Harmony, another concept rife with mystical allusions, maintains a close relationship to resonance and vibration. This established correlation was thought to be quite simply the basis of the hidden order of the immediate, perceivable world, and behind it all were the numbers. It seems that we just can't escape their grip!

Numbers in Music

In addition to his comprehensive historical research, Malkowski also delves into the philosophy of numbers as researched by 20th-century French philosopher R. A. Schwaller de Lubicz. Schwaller's early book *A Study in Numbers* was published in 1917, and examined numbers as not only symbols of expression but also as the purist manner to "convey a cosmogony." Schwaller believed that quantity was critical, but that only when quantity and quality were equal could true harmony be achieved. This homeostatic state would result in an observable, or real, phenomenon. Even consciousness could be described as "a result of the relationship between quantities and the absolute state, where we can conceive of absoluteness only in relation to quantity."

Schwaller also believed that two cosmos existed in one singular universe; one being the absolute, macrocosmic, the other the harmonic microcosmic. He also described this as "quality fragmented and organized into quantity," and Malkowski makes the connection between this worldview and physics, where "there are the immediate and quantum worlds—two very different worlds that exist simultaneously." Schwaller's ideas were certainly ahead of their time, and Malkowski describes his philosophical treatise on numbers as such (obviously mirroring Pythagoras's "All is number" mentality!):

- One: The Monad—The concept of absolute, the unity of all things, the unchanging "all" from which all other numbers are produced. Also known as Chaos, Axis, Tower, Styx, Atlas, and the Throne of Jupiter.
- Two: The Duad—Duality and polarity, the most fundamental aspect of all natural phenomena (not to mention the foundation for Western religious belief in good/evil, light/darkness).

- Three: The Triad—The first odd number after one, and the sacred composition of the monad and duad (think Holy Trinity), the function of which is to create equilibrium between the monad and duad.
- Four: The Tetrad—The "primogenial number," the first born of the combined principles of the three numbers before it. The basis for all nature in that the tetrad is the sum of 1, 2, 3, and 4 = 10, the decad. The number of God. The four elements. The four directions.
- Five: The Pentad—The union between the first even (2) and odd (3) numbers. Symbolized a fifth element known as "ether," and symbolic of nature as the Pentacle or five-pointed star. Pentagrams are considered deeply sacred symbols. Also symbolized the manifest universe.
- Six: The Hexad—The formation of matter into the cosmos, space, and time. Six directions of extension (up, down, left, right, forward, and backward), and the union of the two sexes as in the interlaced triangles of the Star of David or King Solomon's Seal. Male and female, matter and spirit.
- Seven: The Heptad—The mystical nature of Man. The marriage of the threefold nature of mankind (body, mind, and spirit) and the four elements of matter. Also, the combination of the higher principle of the trinity upon the lower four "mortal" principles.
- Eight: The Ogdoad—Renewal and self-replication. A new unity based upon the fact that eight is divided into two 4s, then into two 2s, and then into two 1s.
- Nine: The Ennead—The first square of the first odd number 3. Spiritual and mental achievement, the limit of all numbers for all other numbers come from the first nine, yet can create an infinite amount of new numbers.

- Ten: The Decad—Comprising all arithmetic and harmonic proportions. The number that perfects all others. Within 10, all nature exists, the root source of eternal nature.

These ten numbers form the basis of the Pythagoreans' philosophy, represented in the "tetractys," four rows totaling 10 dots where, according to Malkowski, "the three higher numbers represent the invisible, metaphysical world, and the lower seven refer to physical phenomena." The bottom level consisted of the four elements of earth, water, air, and fire; the center row was the Three Principles of the Moon, Sun, and Sulfur; and the top two rows, contained by a triangle, were the Two Seeds of the Moon and Sun, topped by the One Fruit or Stone. Each row represented a different experience or reality, "a gradation from more collective to more individual experiences." The One Fruit, or Stone, at the top of the tetractys represented the "Unus Mundus," or the Self, and is the totality of the universe, or the World Soul.

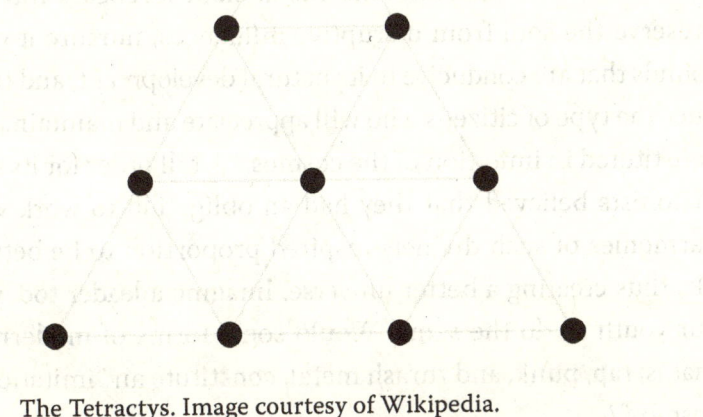

The Tetractys. Image courtesy of Wikipedia.

The Pythagorean cosmology consisted of the two worlds of the Supreme and the Superior, and the lower Inferior World of form, which has three levels similar to the Trinity as a basis of reality. Yet, only in the Inferior World could quantity exist and be measured, and that is the world we live in, where the sacred science of geometry longs to bridge the gap between the lower and upper worlds, as well as the individual souls to the World Soul.

In his book *The Dimensions of Paradise: Sacred Geometry, Ancient Science and the Heavenly Order on Earth,* author and researcher John Michell examines the role of music and proportion in bridging this gap, as well as the strong influence of music on the theories of both Plato and Pythagoras. He begins by looking at Plato's theory of education, which posits that "children must be exposed from their earliest days to the influence of harmonious proportions in everything around them, so that they will grow up with a sense of proportion and the ability to distinguish between the good and the meretricious."

Musical intervals, Michell states, can be expressed as ratios between numbers, thus creating a sort of "numerical canon" that is the composition behind the World Soul. From this canon, musical scales evolved. "By forbidding 'noise' as non canonical music," Michell continues, "Plato and his ancient forebears intended to preserve the soul from disruptive influences, nurture it on those sounds that are conducive to its natural development, and thus produce the type of citizens who will appreciate and maintain a society constituted in imitation of the cosmos." A tall order for its citizens, Platonists believed that they had an obligation to work with the harmonies of such divinely inspired proportion to be better people, thus creating a better universe. Imagine a leader today asking our youth to do the same. Would some forms of modern music, that is, rap, punk, and thrash metal, constitute an "imitation of the cosmos"?

As Michell points out, Plato strongly believed that the secrets of the universe were to be found not by setting one's eyes up to the heavens, but by examining in detail the "precise proportion of number." In addition to the harmonies it inspired, this proportion could only truly be understood through numerical analysis, which Michell's book delves into a bit more deeply than we shall here. Basically, behind the harmonies and chords and scales that were thought to be of a positive, or divine, nature, there were numbers and sequences of numbers that combined to make up notes and half-notes, intervals and octaves, fourths and fifths, and everything in between.

Harmonic proportion, one of the three recognized types of proportions (arithmetic and geometric being the others), was deeply understood by Pythagoreans. Their knowledge carried on a sacred science, which began in civilizations from far more ancient times. As Michell states, "Timaeus" is identified as the earliest account of the three proportion types as part of Pythagorean music theory, "where Plato describes the numerical creation of the physical universe and the soul that binds and animates it."

Plato believed that the World Soul was created out of a range of four octaves. Furthermore, he said that there was a specific number code that served as the root of all natural and philosophical reality (which we will examine in a later chapter). Ironically, through time, scholars have continued to disagree as to what that exact number code is. Michell and others suggest that the first 12 numbers are the basic foundation of creation. These numbers, though, were adapted through time to the units of measurement that a musician playing a wind or string instrument would produce as sound, depending upon the length of pipe or string utilized. Anyone who has ever studied modern music theory, or even tried to learn to read music, knows that precision and measurement play important roles in the nature and quality of the sounds produced. Even the human ear can discern a lovely chord from a distinctly brain-shattering cacophony.

According to Heath's *Sacred Number and the Origins of Civilization*, musical harmony is comprised of the most fundamental of numbers, 1 through 6, and that "musical ratios are the irreducible elements without any common factors taken out." His book extensively describes the harmonic ratios and octaves created by the numbers 1 through 12, and why these special combinations and ratios form the foundation of musical structure, a structure with a parallel in the very resonances of the earth, stars, and planets that make up the cosmos. These ratios may even govern and influence the resonances that we, as humans, vibrate in accordance with.

Heath pays particular attention to the importance of certain prime numbers. "A very important principle emerges within the field of number as it evolves what is, to us, harmony. As stated, the prime numbers 2, 3, and 5 are responsible for the principle of harmony; this means that all the higher primes are fated to occupy the voids left by the field of harmony." Even the prime numbers 7 and 11 have a critical role in the formation of "primary creation," because, as Heath points out, the ratio between the Earth's mean radius and its meridian is 22/7, or two times 11/7, thus giving the two numbers a special place in the hearts and minds of ancient civilizations who linked musical harmony with that of the planets and stars.

Metrology

This serves as the foundational platform for the scientific disciple known as "metrology," which Heath describes as "similarly structured to find the units that maintain simplicity of relationship between different dimensions of built or implied circles." He ascribes this same simplicity as the manner by which ancients transmitted knowledge via the building and study of monuments and temples that were built in accordance with this worldview—think of Stonehenge and its circular shape. Heath calls this association of number and harmony, which was seemingly known and utilized by the ancients, the "metrological application," and its impact can clearly be seen in the architecture of old.

Heath, Michell, and John Neal, also an expert in the area of metrology, all come to similar conclusions about the importance of harmonics in relation to the physical shape of the earth. Neal and Michell discovered "grid constants" that reveal, as Heath puts it, "that the shape of the Earth is related to the harmonic products of the first 25 numbers, seen from the perspective of harmony, and employing only those prime numbers below 12." Michell and Neal's grid constants found a relationship between variations in ancient measurements, approximations to pi used in ancient times, and the ratios found at the end of the series from 1 to 25 with 2, 3, 5, 7, and 11 as "harmonically generative" primes.

The genesis of metrology may have begun with the simple measurement of the English foot and its many ancient variations, all of which related to the size and shape of our planet. However, as Heath points out, the ancients measured things within a "created scheme or order." Today, we measure things as they are actually found in approximation to reality. What you see is what you get. This may tell us why sacred geometry is considered a "science" of the past, but one that still holds great mystery and intrigue today, when our true understanding of reality is based entirely on what we experience right in front of us, and rarely on what is occurring beneath the surface, or beyond the veil.

Much of the worldview upon which sacred geometry is based can be traced back to concepts forged by the likes of Lao Tsu, author of the *Tao Te Ching*, and even to Socrates, mentor of Plato. Both agreed that the whole of creation was divided into three parts (also a basis for the Trinity of Catholicism, as we shall discuss in a future chapter): creation as entirety was the first part; the division of the whole was the second part; and, finally, the interconnectedness between the whole and the parts was part three. From this foundation, all other numbers and number fields supposedly sprang forth. Nowhere is this more obvious than in the yin and yang symbol of Tao, which shows the whole of the circle, the division into white and black halves, and the interconnectedness of the contrary smaller circles within.

This belief in the sacredness of all of creation's foundational structure was clearly evident, and quite obvious in architectural objects. Of all the elements comprising sacred geometry, architecture—whether the building of a crude stone megalith or a precise and intricately detailed chapel—stood as the most profound manner by which man could somehow emulate the divine patterns of the heavens—right here on Earth. Even today, these sacred structures elicit a deep and lasting impression upon those who view them.

In the classic *Philebus* (often called "The Philebus"), one of the last Socratic dialogues of Plato, Socrates talks of the connection between beauty and form:

> I do not mean by beauty of form such beauty as that of animals or pictures, which many would suppose to be my meaning, but, says the argument, understand me to mean straight lines and circles, and the plane or solid figures which are formed out of them by turning-lathes and rulers and measures of angles; for these I affirm to be not only relatively beautiful, like other things, but they are eternally and absolutely beautiful, and they have peculiar pleasure, quite unlike the pleasures of scratching.

The dialogue's central question concerns the relative value of pleasure and understanding, as well as producing a model for thinking about how complex structures are developed. Called "philosophical geometry," this concept also served as the basis for the sacred geometry we study today.

PLATONIC SOLIDS

To start the discussion of form and beauty with Plato again, let's review the five perfect three-dimensional shapes that came to be known as the Platonic Solids.

Tetrahedron—4 faces, 4 vertices, 6 edges

Hexahedron (cube)—6 faces, 8 vertices, 12 edges

Octahedron—8 faces, 6 vertices, 12 edges

Dodecahedron—12 faces, 20 vertices, 30 edges

Icosahedron—20 faces, 12 vertices, 30 edges

A Platonic Solid is basically a convex regular polyhedron; its name is derived from the total number of its faces. The beauty of Platonic Solids lies in their symmetry and angles. Because of this, they have long been regarded as sacred. Although some scholars argue that the octahedron and icosahedron may have been the discovery of Plato's contemporary, Theaetetus, who also may be responsible for determining that there are no other convex regular polyhedra, it was in fact Plato who associated four of the solids with the four classical elements of earth (hexahedron), water (icosahedron), air (octahedron), and fire (tetrahedron).

A convex polyhedron can only be a Platonic solid if:

- All its faces are congruent convex regular polygons.
- None of its faces intersect except at their edges.
- The same number of faces meet at each of its vertices.

In the mid-1980s, University of Chicago professor Robert J. Moon managed to prove that the entire periodic table of elements, of which the entire physical world is comprised, is based upon the five Platonic Solids. Moon also proposed a geometric ordering of the atomic nucleus, inspired by Johannes Kepler's conception of the solar system, as described in Kepler's *Mysterium Cosmographicum*.

Interestingly, Kepler himself tried to apply the five Platonic Solids to the five known non-Earth planets at the time—Mercury, Venus, Mars, Jupiter, and Saturn—but was unable to make the connection work. His model of the solar system was his attempt at a physical correspondence—the innermost layer was the octahedron, the next layer was the icosahedron, the next layer was the dodecahedron, the next was the tetrahedron, and finally the last was the hexahedron, or cube. But all it served to do was inspire his new discovery of the Kepler solids, and the understanding that planetary orbits are not circles. Both of these attempts served as the foundation for his famous Laws of Planetary Motion and an excellent example of failure leading to greater success!

Proportional harmony, Platonic Solids, and sacred constants all come together most visibly in the architecture of Ancient Egypt, India, the area once known as Mesoamerica, Easter Island, and even rural England and Wales, places often described as magical and mystical by all who have had the pleasure of walking among their temples, pyramids, megaliths, and monuments. The designers of sacred sites looked to both earth and sky to determine locations, alignments, and even purposes. Nothing was ever built without a purpose, whether that purpose was to better understand our place in the cosmos, or create a new type of energy or level of consciousness, as has been suggested as the true purpose of the Great Pyramid of Giza.

SACRED ARCHITECTURE

Other sacred sites were meant to invite worship, but even they were built with a divine connection to location in mind. The history of sacred architecture is paralleled by the history of religious architecture, symbolism, and use of motif, with some buildings purposely rendered huge and public, while others were small, private places intended for more personal modes of meditation and reflection. In his article "The Boundary Between the Physical and the Spiritual," architect Norman L. Koonce suggested that sacred architecture served to "make transparent the boundary between matter and mind, flesh and the spirit," and this intention is apparent throughout the ancient world. In his inspiring and beautiful book *The Architecture of Happiness*, Alain de Botton states, "Belief in the significance of architecture is premised on the notion that we are, for better or for worse, different people in different places—and on the conviction that it is architecture's task to render vivid to us who we might ideally be."

Although it might seem blasphemous, the idea that humankind might somehow be equal to the gods (or, at the very least, able to access their wisdom and guidance) serves as the structural foundation for sacred geometry.

Not surprisingly, dozens of books have been written about the lineage and age of the Great Pyramid of Giza, the means of construction for the Pyramid, and even its overall purpose. Some of the more creative theories definitely seem to stretch the limits of believability. In fact, the somewhat derogatory term "Pyramidiot" has been penned to describe opponents to the hard-line, fixed paradigms.

John Michell states in *The Dimensions of Paradise*, "The pyramid, of course, was no mere mathematical model, but an example of the cosmic temple whose traditional function was to procure fusion between upper and lower elements."

Just for starters, here is but a small sampling of the enigmatic number mysteries that the Pyramid contains:

- The ratio of the diameter of the middle of the earth is 11, and the distance between the center of the earth and the center of the moon as 7 is the exact ratio built into the Great Pyramid of Giza (Heath).
- The height times the base length, in English feet, is the length of the degree of latitude for the Pyramid at Giza at 30 degrees North (Neal).
- The cubic capacity of the Ark of the Covenant (71,282 cubic inches) is incredibly similar to the cubic capacity of the stone vessel knows as "Pharaoh Cheops' Sarcophagus" in the King's Chamber (71,290 cubic inches), which has led some researchers to suggest that the Ark was once encased in the Sarcophagus.
- The builders of the Pyramid were apparently aware of the Pythagorean theorem, of the relationship among the sides of a 3:4:5 (right) triangle, and they had knowledge of the concept of pi (Malkowski).
- The accuracy and precision of the construction prompted engineering expert Christopher Dunn to proclaim in his 1998 book *The Giza Power Plant*, after closely examining the Pyramid for two decades, that "the Great Pyramid is the largest, most precisely built, and most accurately aligned building ever constructed in the world."

- The angle of the slopes of the sides is a ratio of 10:9, thus for every 10-foot ascent up the slope of the Pyramid, you rise an altitude of 9 feet. Multiply the altitude of the Pyramid by 10 raised to the 9th power, and you get 91,840,000 miles—the distance from the earth to the sun.
- A pyramid inch is .001 inch larger than an English inch. There are 24 pyramid inches in a cubit, and there are 365.24 cubits in the square base of the Pyramid. There are also 365.24 days in a calendar year.

According to Marshall Payn, author of "The Case for Advanced Technology in the Great Pyramid," in the book *Forbidden History*, the Great Pyramid's builders most likely looked to the stars and astronomy for their precise measurements in construction. Even slight inaccuracies could not be dismissed, Payn suggests, pointing to the minute differences in some measurements of the Pyramid's height in feet that closely match the polar radius of the earth when incorporated into a formula, whereby the base perimeter is equal to one half of a degree of equatorial longitude. The result proved to be off by only a difference of twenty-seven miles, yielding an accuracy of 99.3 percent for the ancient Egyptian builders. Even with the advent of modern-day GPS, that difference is considered negligible, and certainly incredible considering the circumstances!

Payn also points to the importance of the number 43,200, which mythologist and scholar Joseph Campbell traced to the original myths of various ancient cultures (he even traced it to Neolithic times). This figure is even more remarkable when we learn that the Great Pyramid's scale is 2 × 60 × 360, which equals 43,200.

The Great Pyramid is in no way an exclusive sacred portal of sorts between earth and heaven. Even the Temple of Luxor speaks of sacred geometric proportions. Again, we turn to R. A. Schwaller de Lubicz, who superimposed a human skeleton over a drawing of the temple to show how sacred geometric proportions were at play. As outlined in his seminal book, *The Temple of Man*, Schwaller posits that the Golden Section was widely used in the construction of the Temple of Luxor. He believed very strongly that this temple was built to actually contain and encode a system of knowledge within its architectural symbolism.

This "science of correspondences," also attributed to 18th-century Emanuel Swedenborg, a Swedish scientist, philosopher, Christian mystic, and theologian, was deeply understood by the ancients, but has effectively been considered a lost art and science today. Swedenborg believed that "the most ancient people, who were celestial men, thought from correspondence itself, as the angels do," and wrote extensively in his book, *Heaven and Hell*, about the correspondence and connection between the natural world and the spiritual world.

One such place that elicits an ethereal, spiritual feeling is the Stonehenge-Avebury Complex. Everyone has heard of Stonehenge, the circle of massive stones in England's Wiltshire County, built throughout a period of 3,000 years (the standing stones as early as 2000 BC, the bank and ditch approximately 3100 BC) that supposedly encode astronomical and cosmological knowledge in their placement and purpose.

You may be interested to know that Stonehenge, though, is not Britain's largest, or even most important, monument. To the direct north is the largest "henge" monument in the country: Avebury. Interestingly, Avebury was built upon what is known as the "Michael Line." The Michael Line is an invisible geographic line that connects sanctuaries dedicated to St. Michael (more on this later). Henge monuments are traditionally defined as "circular banked enclosures with an internal ditch," according to Wikipedia, and archaeologists have long recognized them as a classic form of sacred earthwork. Despite its bank being inside its ditch, Stonehenge is grouped into such monuments for its "standing stone circle" formation.

Avebury, along with Stonehenge and other key sacred locations, form a triangle in the landscape that, according to John Michell, suggest a ground-based model of the "three key radii of Earth." The key unit is 1,728 feet, equaling 72 Roman feet, and one-fourth the radius of nearby Silbury Hill, another point in the landscape triangle. Michell also compares Stonehenge's ground plan with that of the city of "New Jerusalem," described in Saint John's book of Revelation, and with the mystical 12 hides (measurements of land) of Glastonbury, defined as the area of land able to support a farmer and his family, and equal to 1,440 acres. Stonehenge, when overlaid upon a diagram of the city of New Jerusalem (as envisioned by Saint John) can be seen as a square 7,920 feet wide, and an inner circle of 14,400 cubits around. The dimensions, Michell states, are on a scale of 1:100. "The outer circle," he posits, "has the same perimeter as the square, 316.8 feet. Stonehenge is thus founded on the classic image of sacred geometry, the squared circle representing the reconciliation of opposites, which is the common feature of temples and foundation myths the world over."

St. Mary's Chapel at Glastonbury also features a similar measurement, with the perimeter of its square measuring 316.8 feet with a diameter of 79.2 feet. Michell's book also shows the diameter of an inner circle representing earth at 7,920 miles; the perimeter of the outer circle and square as 31,680 miles. These numbers, as we shall learn later, hold a special sacred spot in the "pattern of the heavens."

The ancient "heavenly city" of New Jerusalem of Saint John the Divine in the book of Revelation is suggested by Michell as the "eternal standard" by which all other sacred structures should be measured, judged, and even copied. "In the symbolism of all religions, a geometric construction representing the heavenly city or map of paradise has a central place," Michell writes. "It occurs in sacred art as a mandala, a concentric arrangement of circles, squares and polygons depicting in essence the entire universe." These sacred places were thought to be a fixed constant in a constantly changing world, a representation of that which never changes. Many have speculated that these arrangements also served to exert a calming, ordering influence on civilization.

In Revelation, Saint John actually describes the measurements by which this heavenly city would be constructed. "And the city lieth foursquare and the length is as large as the breadth; and he measured the city with the reed, 12,000 furlongs. The length and the breadth and the height of it are equal . . . and he measured the wall thereof, an hundred and 40 and 4 cubits. . . ." Michell did the math, so to speak, arriving at specific measurements that took the form of a cube with 12 sides each, 12,000 furlongs, six faces, 144 million square furlongs, and a wall of 144 cubits. He does point out the discrepancy in scales used, as a furlong is 660 feet and a cubit 1.5 feet. But "the basic plan of the New Jerusalem is a square of 12 furlongs containing a circle of 14,4000 cubits." In feet, the diameter of the New Jerusalem circle within the square is 7,920 feet. The earth's diameter in the square is 7,920 miles. The circumferences of both the New Jerusalem and the earth measure 24,883.2 feet and miles, respectively, and the perimeter of the outer square are 31,680 feet and 31,680 miles, respectively.

No matter the numbers, the whole idea was to match the measurement of what was being constructed upon the earth with the earth itself, as if in homage. Perhaps it was also an attempt to reign in the power of the earth's harmonics and resonance by creating a microcosmic "earth" as a city. The idea behind the city of New Jerusalem was obviously an attempt to bridge the gap between "as above, so below." This pattern became the blueprint for other sacred sites, many of which, such as Stonehenge and Avebury, were spaced equidistant along a very magical line.

LEY LINES

The St. Michael Line that joins Avebury, one of the largest Neolithic henge monuments in Europe dating back as far as 5,000 BC, to Stonehenge and other noted sacred sites is called a "ley line," a straight alignment that measures across England from Cornwall to East Anglia. Discovered by John Michell, the St. Michael Line is said to be the most widely known ley line in the world, linking several "holy" sites devoted to St. Michael. With St. Michael's Mount at the southern tip, the line dissects through the Hurlers stone circle, Glastonbury (site of the Tor megalith), Avebury, and the Wandlebury Stone Ring to Hopton in the north.

Ley lines, leys, or Magic Lines are purported alignments of sacred sites, usually ancient in origin, that connect across a landscape in either a straight or curved line. Ley lines often link marker sites along several miles, and it has been thought that they might possibly follow the paths of prehistoric trading routes.

The so-called "discoverer" of ley lines is considered to be the English businessman Alfred Watkins, who allegedly found evidence of these alignments in June 1921 while studying a map. He noticed that various points of historical interest followed a line that traversed across hilltops and created a pattern of lines across a vast landscape. In his book *The Old Straight Track*, Watkins described a ley line as having "a set of points, chosen from a given set of landmark points, all of which lie within at least an arc of 1/4 degree." He urged readers to "imagine a fairy chain stretched from mountain peak to mountain peak, as far as the eye could reach." This chain linked mounds, circular earthwork, and "high places" of the earth at various spaced locales.

Watkins associated the lines with the Roman messenger god Mercury (Greek Hermes), the god of communication, boundaries, and guide to travelers. Watkins also felt there was a Druidic connection to the ley lines, and later wrote a book entitled the *Ley Hunter's Manual* in the late 1920s. However, it was Dion Fortune, the occultist and author of *The Goat-Foot God* who originated the claim that ley lines held a special power that linked ancient holy sites.

Later, the New Age crowd ascribed a sense of cosmic energy to ley lines, determining that the lines followed a specific grid or pattern in the earth itself. Dowsers and psychics alike claimed to be able to "read" and locate ley lines, which also became linked to the Atlantean mythology courtesy of author John Michell's book, *The View Over Atlantis*.

Allegedly, there are ley lines running across the landscapes of western North America (many linked to Native American sites), the southeastern United States, the Glastonbury-Avalon line in the United Kingdom, the Glasgow lines of Scotland, and the south of France linking various holy sites associated with the Mary Magdalene legend. Wales and Ireland also have their share of ley lines, magical sites, and hot spots of mythical interest. The Nazca lines in South America are considered ley patterns, and these mysterious lines are even said to connect the ancient pyramids of Mexico.

Of course, not everyone believes in the mystical concepts ascribed to ley lines. According to *Skepdic.com*, "There is no evidence for this belief save the usual subjective certainty based on uncontrolled observations by untutored devotees. Nevertheless, advocates claim that the alleged energy is connected to changes in magnetic fields. None of this has been scientifically verified."

Are ley lines simply random? Those lines that are actually straight (most are not) can be shown to fall within expected chance occurrence on a map of a heavily populated area, especially when features no longer in existence can be included.

A similar notion was developed by the ancient Chinese far before the English came up with it. The Chinese called their lines "dragon tracks," and they used them for weather forecasting. They were somewhat less successful in that field than today's average meteorologist.

Regardless of the lack of scientific evidence either for or against ley lines, a new, emerging area of archeology called "geodesy" has formed, which incorporates geological surveying as a factor. This modality suggests that these lines are nothing more than humankind's attempts to mark surveying lines, property and boundary markers, as well as the most commonly traveled trade and migration routes.

Watkins himself never attributed any metaphysical or supernatural meaning to ley lines; however, the belief persists today that lines of energy that resonate in the same electromagnetic vibrational frequency as the earth itself mark the landscape and speak of an ancient knowledge far superior to our own. No matter what the origin of these lines, it is really the sites to which they point that continue to intrigue those interested in hidden knowledge and the power and symbolism of numbers.

One of the most interesting end points of ley lines is the famous Rosslyn Chapel, itself a remarkable display of sacred geometry and the use of symbol, harmonics, and numbers to convey a sense of otherworldliness and a divine connection.

Rosslyn Chapel is a 15th-century chapel designed by William Sinclair of the St. Clair family of Scottish nobles descended from the Norman knights, and some claim, linked to the Knights Templar. Originally known as the Collegiate Chapel of St. Matthew, Rosslyn has gained notoriety from the recent bestselling book and movie *The Da Vinci Code* by Dan Brown, which served to further inextricably link it to the legend of the Holy Grail. Many historians and esotericists even insist the Grail legend itself ends at Rosslyn, where ensconced deep within its walls may lie a secret that only music itself can unlock.

The chapel's construction began in 1440 and lasted for approximately forty years. Throughout its history, Rosslyn Chapel has been associated with mystery and intrigue as well as the occult and hidden knowledge. Such collegiate chapels were intended to be both spiritual and educational places of power and knowledge, but as suggested in a three-volume study by Father Richard Augustine Hay, Rosslyn held even deeper mysteries. Hay was the principle authority of the chapel and St. Clair family. He wrote that Rosslyn was unlike any other house of God's service, and that it was a "most curious work, that which it might be done with greater glory and splendour." Sir William is said to have engaged the services of the best masons and workmen available in Europe at the time to build this magnificent structure. Throughout its history, the chapel has maintained an association with the legendary Knights Templar. According to theologians, that association continues even today.

Many authors and Rosslyn researchers suggest that the west wall of the chapel was intended by design to be a model of Jerusalem's Wailing Wall. In addition, mystical symbols carved into the stone ceiling were reportedly discovered in 2005, which appear to be a musical score. Stuart Mitchell undertook this genius accomplishment, finding codes hidden in 213 cubes in the ceiling. The cubes, when combined, formed a series of patterns that resulted in a one-hour musical accompaniment for 13 medieval prayers!

When the composer also discovered that the stones at the foot of 12 pillars formed a classic 15th-century cadence (three chords at the end of a musical piece), he suggested that the music sounded like a "nursery rhyme," a childlike tune that would have been more fitting of a man like William Sinclair. A man who may have been a great architect, but a lousy musician! Mitchell is himself the son of Thomas Mitchell, who spent more than two decades trying to unravel the musical code on the chapel ceiling. Stuart's recording of the mysterious musical notes is called *The Rosslyn Motet*, and it is his hope, among other researchers, that when played on medieval instruments, it will create a resonant frequency throughout the chapel similar to a Cymatic or Chladni pattern, which form when a sustained note vibrates a sheet of metal covered in a powder. The frequency creates a pattern in the powder, and different musical notes produce different patterns such as rhombuses, flowers, diamonds, hexagons, and other shapes . . . all of which were found on the Rosslyn ceiling cubes!

Many scholars insist that these musical tones and corresponding patterns on the ceiling cubes are far more than just coincidence, and that one day we may be able to unlock a medieval secret by repeatedly playing the proper frequencies. So far, the musical mystery remains just that.

Perhaps William Sinclair was familiar with sacred geometry and harmonics, and utilized them in the building of this magical, mystical chapel. Two of the chapel's pillars are believed by Masons to refer to the pillars of Boaz and Joachim, and there are pictorial references on wall carvings to the Key of Hiram, as well as to certain plant species that are found only in America—and which would not be officially discovered for some one hundred years or more.

Some legends state that a huge treasure of amazing proportions, perhaps the Holy Grail itself, lies hidden in the sealed chambers below the chapel's basement floor. It has been said that within the chapel, three giant medieval chests are filled with shocking contents that might change our entire religious history. Others believe the secret lies within the stone walls themselves, ripe with symbolism and hidden meaning. Perhaps one day, the correct series of musical notes may reveal to us the secrets of Rosslyn.

Chapter 4:4

SIGNS AND SYMBOLS

In a symbol there is concealment and yet revelation: here therefore, by silence and by speech acting together, comes a double significance. In the symbol proper, what we can call a symbol, there is ever, more or less distinctly and directly, some embodiment and revelation of the Infinite; the Infinite is made to blend itself with the Finite, to stand visible, and as it were, attainable there. By symbols, accordingly, is man guided and commanded, made happy, made wretched.

—Thomas Carlyle

"Stop." "No right turn." "Yield." Fortunately for our insurance carriers, most of us are familiar with the various signs and symbols utilized in modern transportation. Although sometimes aggravating, they serve a valuable and important purpose. Throughout millennia, mankind has developed and assigned signs and symbols as representative depictions of nearly everything of significance.

SYMBOLS

The word *symbol* has its roots in the Greek term *symbolon*, which means "contract, token, insignia, and a means of identification."

Symbols are objects, pictures, or other visual representations of ideas, concepts, or abstractions. For example, in the United States,

Canada, Australia, and Great Britain, a red octagon is a symbol for "STOP." And here in the United States and now abroad, a pair of golden arches signifies a burger. Signs and symbols have allowed us to use readily identifiable monikers and icons as representations of the original item.

Signs, symbols, and glyphs have been used for religious and occult purposes from the very beginning of time. Early rock and cave art depictions present a fascinating view into the minds of our prehistoric ancestors. Many theories abound regarding the purpose of these creative signs—some have ascribed them to ceremonial purposes, while others believe that they were utilized as a means to transmit information. Whatever the true explanation, they remain a mysterious and enigmatic part of the human experience.

Religion

Religious use of symbology has likewise been commonly employed throughout history. On a daily basis we are confronted by a virtual cacophony of sacred religious icons such as the Christian cross, the Jewish Star of David, the Islamic crescent, the Buddhist Wheel of Dharma, and so on. With the modern societal belief in cultural and religious diversity, suburbia has an increasing number of billboards and street corners dedicated to churches, synagogues, mosques, and other places of holy worship.

NUMBERS

Even our favorite topic of numbers is not immune from the influence of signs and symbols. Math iconography has generally been used to express mathematical statements in an easily understood, plain language. Lancelet Hogben, the famous English statistician and writer said:

Every meaningful mathematical statement can also be expressed in plain language. Many plain-language statements of mathematical expressions would fill several pages, while to express them in mathematical notation might take as little as one line. One of the ways to achieve this remarkable compression is to use symbols to stand for statements, instructions and so on.

Many of the world's most mysterious and sacred places also employ signs, symbols, and numerology as representative icons. From the ancient to the modern world, such wonders as the Great Pyramid of Giza, Stonehenge, Easter Island, Machu Picchu, the Taj Mahal, and even the Rosslyn Chapel all contain within their very structures symbols purposely inscribed to reveal a higher, secret knowledge to those who are willing to look for them. And more times than not, that knowledge has a connection with numbers.

We even have a symbol for numbers themselves: #. The relationship between symbols and numbers is inescapable.

THE TRIAD

Numbers, whether in plain digit form or represented as arcane symbols, have had a profound influence on religion the world over. One of the most well-known symbols is that of "three"—referred to as a triad.

A triad, a group of three, may refer to:

- Greek philosophy: The Pythagorean symbol for the number 3.
- Music: A set of three notes, most commonly forming a diatonic tertian chord.
- Relationship: A term for a relationship between three people.

- Religious: Three deities commonly associated together; three deities forming a group with common associations; three deities thought of as three phases of one deity; or three entities thought of as aspects of one deity (for example, the "great goddess," or Triple Goddess: grandmother, mother, and daughter; crone, matron, and maiden; and, in Catholicism: father, son, and spirit); triple deities.
- Sociology: A term for a group of three people as a unit of study.

Most notably, the triad holds great importance in many religions, from the most ancient Pagan traditions to modern Taoism and Christianity. The power of "three" is seemingly everywhere!

In fact, every major and minor religious system has a similar triadic concept that does one of two things: (1) describes the nature of reality, or (2) describes the path to enlightenment. Only semantics separate these worldwide concepts from what could be termed a "spiritual unified theory," which can be explored and embraced by people no matter what their claimed religion or belief system.

Cosmology

In the ancient Sumerian culture, cosmology was an integral and important part of daily life. Their cosmology centered on the *Enuma Elish*, an epic poem about the creation of the gods, as well as all other forms in existence. The *Elish* would later become a framework for many themes found in mystical Judaism and Islam. The story begins with Nammu, the primeval sea and Mother of all, who created heaven (*an*) and earth (*ki*). According to the story, when the hard metallic shell of the sky was separated and raised above earth by the God Enlil, a third layer of existence opened up, which has the great waters of Nammu. Thus we have one of the first images of a triadic structure of existence on record. From this triadic primordial mess, the substance of which had been in existence for all eternity, the gods themselves emerged two-by-two, and the parade of creation began.

According to Gerald A. LaRue in *Ancient Myth and Modern Life*, this idea of a three-tiered structure found its way into ancient Greek, Egyptian, and even Hebrew creation myths.

In the Egyptian legend, heaven and earth were separated by water. In the Hebrew myth, it was air. Always the mysterious sort, the Babylonians espoused the "Abyss." These and other similar ancient creation myths would eventually develop into more symbolic descriptions of the universe, such as the Shamanic belief in the Lower World, Middle World, and Upper World, and the much later Christian concept of heaven, hell, and purgatory. Now, if you were paying attention, and not still pondering Mr. Hogben's name, you may have noticed that all of those concepts were based on the triadic system of three.

Paganism and Shamanism

Ancient Paganism and Shamanism suggest that even within the realm of a genderless divinity, there were still three levels of existence with which humans would be forced to contend: the physical, mental, and spiritual. These three could be more easily termed as body, mind, and spirit. Again, the power of three!

Even Neo-Platonists understood this basic Hermetic Law: As Above, So Below. Earth-based religions understood the connection between man, nature, and the creative force behind it all. Using sacred rituals, herbs, chanting, and cadence, Shamans journeyed through the vast realms of the Lower World, where the basest primal existence occurred, the Middle World of day-to-day existence, and the Upper World where superior guidance and knowledge was available. At least 40,000 years before the dawn of Christianity, Shamanic peoples understood that the only way to wholeness and connection with the creative force was to be able to move easily between the Triple Worlds. They believed that in order to enter the realm of pure spirit, they needed the ability to transcend the limits of the physical body and mind.

Were these ideas the precursors of later concepts of God, Man, and Holy Spirit? Were they forerunners of the concepts of Id, Ego, and Superego as introduced by Freud and later reconstructed to indicate the subconscious, conscious, and super conscious? And what about the Buddhist concepts of Personhood, Mindfulness, and Nirvana? Or the metaphysical suggestion of Self, Conscious Awareness, and Higher Self? Even the much more recent concepts of Right Brain/Intuitive, Left Brain/Analytical, and Third Eye/Spiritual may have its underpinnings in these ideas.

Egyptian Beliefs

The ancient myths and stories of creation, including the Egyptian tale of the Reigning Queen as Mother of God, the Reigning Pharaoh as Sun God or Father immanent in the flesh among men, and the Heir Apparent (Prince) as the Son both of God and God to be, all speak of a triadic structure upon which man could understand not only the way the world around him was made, but the way he, himself was made and meant to express his being. This idea of expression would repeat itself throughout history, from Queen, Pharaoh, and Prince/Son; to Buddha, Dharma, Sangha; to God, Christ, and Adam; to Father, Son, and Holy Spirit; to today's popular notion of Me, Myself, and I.

Christianity

Perhaps the most obvious physical Trinity occurs in Christianity, where the Father, Son, and Holy Spirit are first described as actual beings. The Father is God, the Son is the Christ—also called Son of

God and Son of Man—and the Holy Spirit is often described in the New Testament as a "presence, which descended upon" whomever was the lucky chosen. But even the Christian church in its earliest configuration had issues with the simplistic, physical-oriented Trinity. If Jesus was the Son, yet also the Word (*Logos*) made flesh, was he, too, God? Was Christ made of the same nature as God? And who or what was the Holy Spirit?

When the early church bishops gathered at the Council of Nicaea in the year 325 AD, they actually resolved (although there were a few dissenters) this questioning by creating the Apostle's Creed. This historic meeting decided that from that point on, it would be officially stated that the Creator and the Redeemer were one and the same. At this point, the Trinity became less a physical reality and more a spiritual symbol representing a path to divine union, with God as the Father Almighty, the Son of God as Lord Jesus Christ, and the Holy Spirit as the binding agent, so to speak.

Yet even as Christianity developed, and as Gnostic and Mystical Christianity began to grow, the somewhat physical concept of One God, One Son (Jesus), and some mysterious third "entity" named the Holy Spirit began to expand into something more symbolic, and less material. This was likely due in part to the natural evolution of human thought and spiritual unfoldment.

This and other similar thoughts would be echoed in the ancient Eastern wisdom schools as well. *The Bhagavad Gita*, long considered the exemplary text of the Hindu culture, states in its Eighteenth Teaching:

> There is no being on earth
> or among the gods in heaven
> free from the triad of qualities
> that are born of nature.

In his introduction to Barbara Stoler Miller's translation of *The Bhagavad Gita*, Huston Smith states that, "To uncover the nature of the self, the Gita approaches it from three directions that triangulate the self. . . . One of these concerns its makeup, its attributes or qualities. A second distinguishes different spiritual attitudes that serve as starting points for the journey to God . . . the third system of classification turns on differences in what grabs people's interests in the world." All three attributes, as per Huston, create a model of the human self and the psychological and spiritual nature.

Even the various aspects of Krishna's material nature are described as triadic and are analyzed in terms of the three fundamental qualities of lucidity (*sattva*), passion (*rajas*), and dark inertia (*tamas*). These three natural qualities are what constitute, in Hindu thought, the nature of man. Note here the similarities to the Id, Ego, and Superego concept of Freud! Was Freud's famous theory possibly based upon the Hindu teachings?

Looking closely, one can even see a parallel here with the later Christian concept of heaven, hell, and purgatory. Krishna tells Arjuna in the *Gita's* Fourteenth Teaching:

> Men who are lucid go upward;
> men of passion stay in between;
> men of dark inertia,
> caught in vile ways, sink low.

The triadic nature of Hindu faith is also made up of these three elements, inherent in the embodied self, and this trinity of lucidity, passion, and dark inertia presents itself throughout *The Bhagavad Gita* as a symbol of the three levels of man's nature, both physical and spiritual.

Chinese Belief

In the *Tao Te Ching*, the centerpiece of all Chinese religion and philosophy, we see a close parallel between the Tao teaching of *te* (individual soul), *Tao* (universal or cosmic soul), and *chi* (universal energy), and the older Hindu Vedic concept of *atman* (individual soul), *Brahman* (universal soul), and *Moksha* (liberation). *Tao* and *Brahman* both represent Cosmic Unity, or the Father. The individual soul as represented by *te* and *atman* can also be called the Son. And as for the Holy Spirit, we offer *chi* energy present in all things, or for the Vedic Hindus, a pure liberation or freedom of the soul. The Tao teachings of the Yan Hui, one of Confucius's disciples, also include the idea that the human being and cosmos share three life-forces: spirit (*shen*), breath (*qi*), and vital essence (*jing*), also known as the "Three Pure Ones." This personification of the triadic nature of being is echoed in every tradition from the East, with only slight variations in presentation and semantics.

Chinese Buddhism presents the trinity concept as present throughout spiritual teachings as the Three Jewels: Buddha, *Dharma*, and *Sangha*, or the God-Head, his teachings, and his community (also referred to as the Teacher, His Teaching, and the freedom the teachings inspire). These three jewels symbolized the actions to be taken to achieve union with the Divine, and was a common concept throughout Eastern thought; it was even paralleled in the Jain religion with the trinity of *samyag-darsana* (correct perception of insight), *samyagjnana* (correct knowledge), and *samyag-caritra* (correct conduct).

Thich Nhat Hanh emphasizes the need for a budding Buddha to live from the teachings of the Three Jewels, and in his book *Living Buddha, Living Christ* urges those seeking enlightenment to understand that "every moment is an opportunity to breathe life into the Buddha, the *Dharma*, and the *Sangha*. Every moment is an opportunity to manifest the Father, Son, and Holy Spirit." Thus, the concept of Buddha as a physical deity, *Dharma* as a physical reality of right action, and *Sangha* as a physical community or the "body of man" is transformed into symbols of inner transformation, where the inner God uses inner right thought and action to achieve a community of spirit. This is what Hanh means when he emphasizes that we can "touch the living Buddha and the living Christ" within each of us.

In Robert Thurman's translation of the *Tibetan Book of the Dead*, we see a triad appear in the Tibetan Buddhist concept of Three Bodies of Buddhahood: (1) Truth Body, associated with the ultimate reality; (2) Beatific Body, the subjective and transcendent wisdom aspect; and (3) Incarnational Emanation Body, the physical manifestation. In this we see a powerfully obvious match-up with the Christian Trinity of the ultimate Father God, the subjective Holy Spirit that permits transcendence, and the Son who is the physical manifestation that embodies the other two.

Thurman draws a beautiful correspondence between the Buddha bodies and the processes of life (Emanation Body), death (Truth Body), and the Between (Beatific Body). For many Christians of the Western World, these correspondences can also be applied to heaven (Death), earth (Life), and purgatory (what lies between), with Death being the ultimate permanent union with the Divine (and appearing to be somewhat more "superior" than life, at least to the Buddhists!).

Hanh also constantly refers to the parallels between the Buddhist foundational practice of the Three Jewels of Buddha, *Dharma*, and *Sangha*, and the Trinity of the Christian church. The common symbolism is not lost on Hanh, who suggests that just as taking refuge in the Three Jewels is at the foundation of every Buddhist practice, taking refuge in the Trinity is at the foundation of every Christian practice.

Other Ways of the Trinity

Meanwhile, Gnostic Christian texts would bring the feminine face of God into the fray. Author and scholar Elaine Pagels recounts a passage from the Apocryphon of John, which tells of a mystical vision of the Trinity he experienced while grieving for the Crucified Christ: "... and I was afraid, and I saw in the light ... a likeness with multiple forms, and the likeness had three forms." John questions the vision and receives this answer: "I am the one who is with you always. I am the Father; I am the Mother; I am the Son."

Pagels explains that this version of the Trinity is based upon the Hebrew term for spirit, *ruah*, which is a feminine word, thus concluding that the feminine "person" conjoined with the Father and Son must be the Mother. Another feminine Trinity symbol appears in the Gospel according to Philip, which describes the Holy Spirit as Mother and Virgin, consort to the Heavenly Father. Philip believes this is the true account for the Virgin Birth symbolism of Christology, "Christ, therefore, was born from a virgin," meaning from the Holy Spirit, not from a virgin woman named Mary.

Pagels also suggests that Wisdom (Sophia) could have also served as the feminine aspect of the Trinity. Sophia, wisdom, translates a Hebrew feminine term, *hokhmah*, and refers to the saying in Proverbs, "God made the world in Wisdom."

Sefirot

Jewish mystics who studied the Kabbalah also understood the triadic symbolism of their Christian counterparts. It was the Hebrew God Yahweh, after all, that the early Christian Church was trying to define by adding the Trinitarian nature. In the Kabbalah, a more metaphysical understanding of the nature of God, the All, *Ein Sof*, takes form in the three major *sefirot*, or the qualities through which the Divine emanates and performs its actions. The first major emanation is *Keter*, also called *Ayin*, Nothingness. From Keter a second point emanates, *Hokmah* (wisdom) also called *Yesh*, Being. This sefirah is the beginning of being-from-nothingness, the beginning of revelation and existence. The third point of emanation is *Binah*, Understanding, which is required to reveal that which exists. From these three sefirot emerge the six dimensions of providence.

Each group of sefirot is revealed in triads from a sefira before it; for example, *Hesed* (Love) emanated from *Hokhmah* (Wisdom); *Gevurah* (Power) from *Binah* (Understanding); and *Tiferet* (Beauty) from *Keter* (Nothingness). Kabbalists claim that it is improper to probe the essence of the first three sefirot because they constitute the Divine Mind, Wisdom, and Understanding. Note the parallel here with the early Greek Christian Orthodox church's claim that the true nature of the Divine was unexplainable, thus the need for a more symbolic interpretation of the Trinity.

Kabbalah

Kabbalists understood the *Ein Sof* as the Infinite, from which all else emanated, including humankind. In "The Chain of Being" from *The Essential Kabbalah* by Daniel C. Matt we are told, "The entire chain is one. Down to the last link, everything is linked with everything else; so divine essence is below as well as above, in heaven and on earth. There is nothing else." And then, in *"Ein Sof* and You," we learn that "each of us emerges from the *Ein Sof* and is included in it. We live through its dissemination." The *Ein Sof* is the Father of the Christian world. We are the Sons. And the dissemination of the *Ein Sof* is the Holy Spirit that moves in and through us.

As Rabbi Eliazar ben Judah of Worms, Jewish mystic and philosopher, proclaimed in "The Song of Unity" in Gershom Sholem's *Major Trends in Jewish Mysticism*:

> Everything is in Thee and Thou art in everything: Thou fillest everything and dost encompass it: when everything was created Thou was in everything; before everything was created, Thou was everything.

Another concept of Kabbalah is the Supernal Triad. According to the Universal Kabbalah Network (*www.universalkabbalah.net*):

> The Supernal Triad is very much like the Celtic trinity knot; there are three aspects, yet they are all interwoven such that the three are one and the energy flow between them is unbroken. While there are three aspects, they occur simultaneously with Kether being the initial spark, Chokmah being the flame that extends out, and Binah like the holder that contains the flame, allowing its light to emanate out but not its destructiveness.

This triadic concept of unity is very interesting, and, it would seem likely that it has served as the basis for diverse religious iconography. Again, from the Universal Kabbalah Network:

> The supernals are the "3 mothers" associated with the Hebrew Letters Shin (spirit/fire), Aleph (air), and Mem (water), which are also the 3 mother rays of Amon Ra: numbers, letters, and sounds that are used to write the name of God, from which all creation comes. The third ray, Binah (Mem), being the one from which all other rays and creational

energies are birthed or emanated out from. We see this in the Kabbalah by the path that the lightning bolt or "flaming sword" takes as it carries the creational energies down from source to Malkuth. Binah is the last of the supernals that it enters before coming into the lower realms. Thus, Binah is the closest of the supernals to the world of form; hence it is the original archetypal form, whereas Chokmah is the original archetypal force. These roles of form and force can also be explained through the beginning stages of creation.

Unlike its sister religions of Judaism and Christianity, Islam considered the Trinity a blasphemous concept. To the followers of the Koran, trying to speculate on things theologically was referred to, somewhat condescendingly, as *Zanna*. This term translates roughly to "self-indulgent guesswork about things that cannot possibly be known," and perfectly describes their disdain for theological pondering.

The idea of a triadic nature of God was definitely not something Muslims accepted, or would even consider. To the Muslim, God, or Allah, was all, is all, and will always be all there is.

Muhammad the Prophet, who supposedly channeled the Koran in a series of trance states, considered the Koran the word of God directly translated to Arabic. According to the Koran, Allah was indivisible All. This emphasis on total and complete oneness would turn the Islamic churches away from the Trinity doctrine embraced in nearby Christian churches. According to author Karen Armstrong, a former Roman Catholic nun turned religious scholar, the Christian Incarnation of Christ was also blasphemous to the Islamic Church. Instead, the Koran spoke of an impersonal God who cannot be personified, but only glimpsed through signs of nature and contemplation of the Koran itself.

Images of the triune nature of God and reality abound in religious traditions, from ancient Celtic Paganism to Christianity. Top left: a triskele; top right: a trefoil; bottom left: a triquetra; and bottom right: a shield trinity. Images courtesy of Wikipedia Commons.

FAIRY TALES

Remember Goldilocks? She crashed the home of the Three Bears. How about our friend the troll, who made trouble for the Three Billy Goats Gruff? The Three Blind Mice tried to escape an old lady's wrath. The Three Little Pigs learned about the effects of wind on housing materials. Fairy tales, long a staple of folkloric studies, prominently display a preference for certain numbers, namely the number 3. From the three notes played by the Pied Piper, to Cinderella and her two ugly stepsisters, to three wishes, three tasks, and three corners to go around, the prevalence of the number 3 in the stories, which in certain cultures conveyed knowledge, taught lessons, and entertained children all in one fell swoop, cannot be ignored. We can even see this pattern in the Arthurian tales of the quest for the Holy Grail, not to mention the story of the Three Wise Men of the Christian Bible.

Some experts believe this is because of the structure of story itself; every story has a beginning, middle, and end. Within this framework, the story unfolds, as a "hero's journey" of sorts, that involves, as Joseph Campbell once put it, an initiation, a quest, and a resolution. These three stages permit the magic of 3 to appear yet again!

But perhaps it is our Indo-European background that provides us with this triadic pattern. If so, was this designed expressly to challenge the usual dichotomies of good and evil, night and day, black and white, rich and poor, and so on? According to Herb Buckland in "The Number Three—Folklore-Fantasy-Fiction?" if we hold to the Out of Africa theory, it can be suggested that we are all third generational descendants, with Africans being the first line of descendancy, Asians the second, and the Indo-Europeans the third. These cultural explanations parallel the idea that even in the world of science, and our own bodies, we see the triadic pattern, as in our DNA, RNA, and proteins.

There may be a subtler, archetypal reason for the number 3 in fairy tales and stories. With each of the three challenges, the ante is upped, requiring more of our hero or heroine. With each bear or pig, there is a greater problem, and a better solution to solve the problem. Let us not forget our favorite ignoramuses—the three stooges. With each third wish, the chance for three more.... After all, we are the third planet from the sun.

Fairy tales and stories don't just stop at the number 3. Persian legends speak of seven caverns that aspirants must move along during their seventy years on earth. We tell tales of the seven seas. And who can forget *The House of the Seven Gables?* Egyptian legend tells of The Seven Hathors, fairy godmothers that bestow certain fate upon newborn babies. In the Talmud, we have seven stages of a man's life: the infant, the child, the boy, the young man, the married man, the parent, and the old man. Shakespeare wrote of the seven stages of a man's life in his play, *As You Like It*:

The Seven Ages of Man, by William Shakespeare

All the world's a stage,
And all the men and women merely players:
They have their exits and their entrances;
And one man in his time plays many parts,
His acts being seven ages. At first the infant,
Mewling and puking in the nurse's arms.
Then the whining school-boy, with his satchel
And shining morning face, creeping like snail
Unwillingly to school. And then the lover,
Sighing like furnace, with a woeful ballad
Made to his mistress' eyebrow. Then a soldier,
Full of strange oaths, and bearded like the pard,
Jealous in honor, sudden and quick in quarrel,
Seeking the bubble reputation
Even in the cannon's mouth. And then the justice,
In fair round belly with good capon lined,
With eyes severe and beard of formal cut,
Full of wise saws and modern instances;
And so he plays his part. The sixth age shifts
Into the lean and slipper'd pantaloon,

> With spectacles on nose and pouch on side,
> His youthful hose, well saved, a world too wide
> For his shrunk shank; and his big manly voice,
> Turning again toward childish treble, pipes
> And whistles in his sound. Last scene of all,
> That ends this strange eventful history,
> Is second childishness and mere oblivion,
> Sans teeth, sans eyes, sans taste, sans every thing.
> —*As You Like It,* act 2, scene 7

In her book *The Interpretation of Fairy Tales,* psychologist Marie-Louise von Franz suggests that number patterns in fairy tales are clues and may possibly be indicative of ancient patterns of destiny that mark a natural rhythm to events. This rhythmic pattern no doubt applies to our own lives and, as Dame Anita Roddick stated in *Numbers,* there might just be a numeric pattern or combination of patterns that "predict the futures we are hurtling towards."

So there is a reason why the king has three daughters, the cock crows three times, the three little kittens keep losing their mittens, and the three ships sail into the harbor each morning at Christmastime; a reason that cannot be foreseen except in the murky mists of future time.

In addition to our friendly number 3, the numbers 1 and 2 also hold great significance in religious traditions (as well as in mythology and folklore). The number 1 represents the ultimate unity, God, the Divine. This is the number that unites all others into wholeness. One need only think about the symbol of interlocking wedding rings to give the idea of two becoming one, or the Star of David, combining the masculine and feminine triangles in one extraordinarily sacred symbolic image. Even with the importance of this uniting icon, the number 2, representing duality, is present here as well. And the number 3, of such huge importance, cannot exist without these two numbers coming before it, merging to create a complete tri-fold identity. Similar to the yin and yang symbol, the two halves combine to produce the one, whole unit. In the next chapter, we will also look at other numbers of significance; however, when it comes to symbols and signs, few hold the kind of power over us as the first three, literally defining our reality as body, mind, and spirit; earth, water, and sky; birth, life, and death.

5

In occult traditions, the number 5 takes on metaphysical importance, embodying the image of the human body, with limbs outspread, as in the famous Vitruvian Man of da Vinci fame. The pentagram, a mystical prime number that combines the sum of 2 and 3, 1 and 4, has been sacred to Pagans for centuries. The number 5 is prevalent in the stories of the New Testament, with Christ receiving five main wounds to his body at Calvary and feeding the five thousand masses with five loaves of bread. Five represents humanity, and to both ancient Pagans and modern Wiccans, it represents air, fire, water, earth, and spirit—the stuff of which life is made.

The ancient Chinese believed that there were five basic elements that formed the elemental basis for all things: wood, fire, earth, metal, and water. We have five senses, and five digits on each hand and each foot. The pentagram symbol was widely used in magickal practices, and is still considered a sacred occult symbol to those who believe it embodies mankind within its points. But inversely, the pentagram also has a more sinister representation due to its often false association to the satanic religion. The identification with the Pagan god Pan, or the mysterious horned Baphomet, surely did not add to the inverse pentagram's appeal to Christians, who proceeded to label the innocuous image as evil. Pan was a harmless woodland god promoting procreation and good times.

The Bolzani pentacle (left) is a depiction of Christ the man as a macrocosmic whole. The inverse pentagram of Eliphas Levi represents the Goat God Baphomet of occult tradition. Images courtesy of Wikipedia.

Baphomet? The creation of occultist Eliphas Levi in his *Dogma and Rituals of High Magic,* in which he included an image he had drawn himself that he described as Baphomet and "The Sabbatic Goat," a winged humanoid goat with breasts and a torch on its head between its horns. Strangely, though, in Levi's original drawings, the pentagram was not inverted. Yet Baphomet worship was linked to the Templars and even the Freemasons, which may have lent more ammunition to devout Christians looking to undermine secret societies with metaphysical teachings.

Regardless of one's personal beliefs or convictions, the power of numbers and symbols have shaped our beliefs to the point where everyone on earth recognizes the positive elements of a star, and the negative elements of that star turned on its tip.

Today we see the symbolic use of numbers to represent "something else" at work, albeit in a more streetwise manner. Take modern public safety professionals, for example. Police officers, firefighters, and EMS personnel all use number codes to convey information about certain crimes, behaviors, status, even their own physical locations. Interestingly, street gangs have developed a number-related code of their own, as a means of communicating, as their law enforcement counterparts do, without really saying what they mean to say. It's a form of shorthand for the select few to understand, just as, perhaps, the numeric codes evident in legends, myths, and tales of old.

Numbers are such an integral part of our society, and have come to represent and symbolize so much. Ever since man first learned to measure and specify quantity, we have been on a progressively increasing path. It is only natural that numbers have taken on symbolic significance in image form—the form we humans best relate to and understand. Perhaps Sergeant Joe Friday's famous catchphrase "Just the facts, ma'am" should have been "Just the numbers, ma'am."

Chapter 5:5

MYSTERY NUMBERS

The creator of the Universe works in mysterious ways. But he uses a base 10 counting system and likes round numbers.
—Scott Adams (American Cartoonist)

On a regular day, the average human experiences hundreds, if not thousands, of events—some big and bold, others trivial and forgettable, but all involving numbers. As we have made clear in previous chapters, for many, a particular number or numbers will show up time and time again. Often, this seeming coincidence infuses a deeper meaning, or a greater mystery into our normally mundane existence. Mystery numbers suit up and show up a little more often than their neighbors. They get noticed. They stand out.

Similar to the lead characters in the popular book and movie *The Da Vinci Code*, we notice them, popping up in the least, and sometimes the most, likely of places, and akin to Robert Langdon, we shake our heads in confusion at their persistence. We cannot escape them.

Perhaps we should call them the "Pythagoras Code."

13

To some, this simple number that follows 12 strikes horror into the heart and fear into the darkest corners of the soul. Unlucky number 13 means black cats and broken mirrors, shadows not to be crossed over, ladders not to be walked under, and cracks not to be stepped upon (lest you wanna break your momma's back). How on earth did 13 get such a bad rap anyway? The number is so bad it has even garnered itself its own phobia—triskaidekaphobia. According to Wikipedia, "Triskaidekaphobia (from Greek tris=three, kai=and, deka=ten) is an irrational fear of the number 13; it is a superstition and related to a specific fear of Friday the 13th, called paraskevidekatriaphobia or friggatriskaidekaphobia."

Some hotels and buildings won't even label the floors between 12 and 14. Others refuse to leave their homes on the 13th of each month, most notably on any Friday the 13th, when unspeakable horrors might occur. On some passenger aircraft, such as those of Continental Airlines, Air New Zealand, Alitalia, and Meridiana, you never have to worry about being assigned that unlucky seat number because it is not available.

When it comes to explaining why we hate the number 13, there are many theories and beliefs. One, posited by landscape designer and architect Charles A. Platt in 1925, suggests that 13 is the first number that a person is unable to count to using their eight fingers, two thumbs, and two feet. This rather farfetched explanation is matched by suggestions that 13 is unlucky because it is the number of full moons in a year, or because it is a number unable to be paired or mated, or even because Judas Iscariot was the 13th person to sit down to dinner before he betrayed Jesus Christ.

Other explanations refer to the number before it, 12, as the number of wholeness or completeness, as indicated in the 12 Apostles of Christ, the 12 signs of the zodiac, and the 12 months in a year. The number 12 also adds up in single digits to 3, the trinity number, which, as we saw in the previous chapter, holds great influence and power in religious traditions and metaphysics alike. There were 12 knights in King Arthur's Round Table, 12 days of Yule, 12 disciples each to Buddha and Mithra, 12 descendants of Allah and 12 tribes of Israel, 12 paladins of Charlemagne, and 12 fruits of the spirit. There are 12 inches in a foot and 12 fruits on the Cosmic Tree.

No wonder poor 13 is the odd-man-out, the leftover, and the rebel.

In a *National Geographic* article titled "Friday the 13th Phobia Rooted in Ancient History," John Roach and Donald Dossey, founder of the Stress Management Center and Phobia Institute in Asheville, North Carolina, and a folklore historian who authored *Holiday Folklore, Phobias and Fun*, said fear of Friday the 13th is rooted in ancient, separate bad-luck associations with the number 13 and the day Friday. The two unlucky entities ultimately combined to make one super bad unlucky day. Dossey traces the fear of 13 to a Norse myth about 12 gods having a dinner party in Valhalla, their heaven. In walked the uninvited 13th guest, the mischievous Loki. Once there, Loki arranged for Hoder, the blind god of darkness, to shoot Balder the Beautiful, the god of joy and gladness, with a mistletoe-tipped arrow.

"Balder died and the whole Earth got dark. The whole Earth mourned. It was a bad, unlucky day," said Dossey. From that moment on, Dossey states, the number 13 has been considered ominous and foreboding.

We authors prefer a simpler explanation for the horror behind the number 13: it is the number that indicates the age when a child becomes a teenager.

Despite its bad rap, especially on Fridays in countries such as Sweden, Belgium, and Germany (Tuesdays in Greece and Spain), there are just as many indicators of the uniquely positive qualities of the number 13. It is the number of the 13 Attributes of Mercy in the Torah. Thirteen is the number of the original colonies that the United States was founded upon. It is the number of loaves in a baker's dozen (or donuts, if you prefer). It is also a prime number *and* a Fibonacci number, thus proving that what is bad to some is good to others, and that even with numbers, it is all a matter of perspective and belief.

In the Kabbalah, the number 13 is the value of unity, Achad, which is Hebrew for "one." According to Rabbi Michael Berg's book *The Way: Using the Wisdom of Kabbalah for Spiritual Transformation and Fulfillment,* "The number 13 holds great significance according to Kabbalah. The Hebrew words for 'love' (ahava), 'care' (de'aga), and 'one' (echad) all have the numerical value of 13. In addition, kabbalistically, the number 13 indicates the ability to rise above the influence of the 12 signs of the Zodiac (12 + 1 = 13), not being bound by the influences of the cosmos."

More down to earth is the influence of this number on something we all worship and adore: money.

The U.S. $1 bill has the following on the back:

- 13 steps on the pyramid.
- The motto above the pyramid has 13 letters (annuit coeptis).
- *E pluribus unum,* written on the ribbon in the eagle's beak, has 13 letters.
- 13 stars appear over the eagle's head.
- 13 stripes are on the shield.
- 13 war arrows are in the eagle's right talon.
- The olive branch in the eagle's left talon has 13 leaves.

So, if the fear of the number 13 is a part of your belief system, we ask that you send all dollar bills to us via our website post office box address.

In their book, *The United Symbolism of America: Deciphering Hidden Meanings in America's Most Familiar Art, Architecture, and Logos,* authors Robert Hieronimus, PhD, and Laura Cortner come to the defense of number 13. They state that the misunderstanding of this innocent number is a recent phenomenon, appearing to be a "strange leftover from the superstitions of the Dark Ages." According to them, it began when the Church started its persecution of women and Pagan healers. "The number 13 is associated with the followers of the Goddess and the way this culture marked time, based on the annual menstruation cycle of the average woman." The authors contend that the word spread that the number 13 was evil, and the Pagan healers suffered by being burned at the stake as witches.

Yet, as the authors point out, these same "holy persecutors" failed to recognize the importance of the number 13 in their own Bible, a number mentioned even as far back as the book of Genesis. Before this negative connotation was attached, the number 13 was, according to Hieronimus and Cortner, "seen as a number of transformation, symbolizing renewal, rebirth, and regeneration. This interpretation may have resulted from the fact that 13 follows that nice, round, complete number of a dozen." They also point to the repeated use of the number by our nation's Founding Fathers, who must have understood its importance in the repeated symbolism of the Great Seal and the American Flag of our original colonies.

7

Superstition is one of the prime culprits to blame for negative values attributed to any number. The same goes for good values. Did you know that the number 7 is considered in many cultures to be the luckiest number of all?

In the Old and New Testament of the Bible, the number 7 shows up dozens of times: seven days warning for Noah before the flood; seven locks of hair on Samson's head; seven daughters of Jethro in Exodus; seven priests with seven trumpets on the seventh day in

Joshua 6:4; seven devils possessing Mary Magdalene; seven sons of the priest Sceva in Acts 19:14.

In the book of Revelations, the vision of St. John the Divine, the number 7 appears repeatedly: seven churches; seven spirits; seven golden candlesticks; seven stars, angels, lamps, seals, horns, eyes, trumpets, thunders, crowns, plagues, vials, mountains, and kings. The number 7 obviously held a reverent position in the Judeo-Christian traditions. Other numbers do appear frequently in the Bible as well, but certainly not with the repetitive nature of 7. In occult symbology, the number 7 is considered deeply sacred, oft considered the number of the spirit of "all," or "the everything."

In the Jewish religion, the number 7 plays a significant role. According to Rabbi Yaakov Salomon, writing for *Aish.com*:

> The fact that the Torah begins with a verse containing 7 words and 28 letters (divisible by 7) is hardly remarkable. But when placed within the context of the overwhelming number of associations in Judaism with 7, a fascinating tapestry begins to unfurl. Kabbalah teaches that 7 represents wholeness and completion. After seven days, the world was complete. There are 6 directions in our world: north, south, east, west, up, and down. Add to that the place where you are, and you have a total of seven points of reference.

A few examples of the number 7 in the Jewish religion:

- Shabbat is the seventh day of the week.
- In Israel, there are seven days of Passover and Sukkot.
- When a close relative dies, we sit Shiva for seven days.
- Moses was born and died on the same day—the seventh of Adar.

- The Menorah in the Temple had seven branches.
- There are seven holidays in the Jewish year: Rosh Hashana, Yom Kippur, Sukkot, Chanukah, Purim, Passover, and Shavuot.
- At every Jewish wedding, seven blessings are recited (Sheva Brachot).
- Moses was the seventh generation after Abraham.
- Each plague in Egypt lasted seven days.
- God created seven levels of heaven. (Hence the expression, "I'm in seventh heaven!")
- The Jewish calendar, largely lunar, has a cycle of intercalation that contains seven leap years during each nineteen-year period.
- The Talmud lists seven female prophets: Sarah, Miriam, Deborah, Hannah, Avigail, Chuldah, and Esther.

Pythagoreans called 7 the perfect number, 3 and 4, the triangle and the square, the perfect figures. Philo of Alexandria, a contemporary of Christ, said, "Nature delights in the number 7," recognizing its significance in the number of notes in music, stars in the Great Bear, and stages of the life of a man. Seven is the number of external holes in the human head: two eyes, two nostrils, one mouth, and two ears. Seven is the smallest positive integer whose name in English is more than one syllable long. The United States Constitution, as drafted in Philadelphia in 1787, was composed of seven Articles. The United States declared independence in the seventh month of 1776.

There were traditionally seven wonders of the ancient world, though only the Great Pyramid of Egypt still stands today. There were seven seas, and there are seven chakras, seven basic principles of bushido, and seven points on a sheriff's star (the heptagram, or seven-pointed star is a traditional symbol for warding off evil). Roll

The number 7 plays a significant role in religion and mythology.

Christianity

- The seven sacraments in the Christian faith (though some traditions assign a different number).
- The seven churches of Asia to which the book of Revelation is addressed.
- The seven joys of the Virgin Mary, of Roman Catholic, Anglican, and other traditions.
- The seven sorrows of the Virgin Mary, of Roman Catholic, Anglican, and other traditions.
- The seven corporal acts of mercy of Roman Catholic, Anglican, and other traditions.
- The seven last words (or seven last sayings) of Jesus on the cross.
- The seven virtues: chastity, temperance, charity, diligence, kindness, patience, and humility.
- The seven deadly sins: lust, gluttony, greed, sloth, wrath, envy, and pride.
- The seven terraces of Mount Purgatory (one per deadly sin).

a 7 in Vegas and you are bound to go home with some cash in your pocket. Even one type of ladybug, considered a lucky friend to all gardeners, has seven spots.

Even the Freemasons worshipped the number 7, so to speak. On a Scottish Mason's apron, there are seven tassels on each side. King Solomon took seven years to build his temple, which was dedicated to the glory of God in the seventh month in a festival that lasted seven days. There are seven liberal arts and sciences, which is a traditional Masonic concept. Masons require seven Brethren to make a Lodge perfect, and must have seven steps on the winding

- In the genealogy in the Gospel of Luke, Jesus is 77th in a direct line.
- The number of heads of the three beasts ($7 \times 10 \times 7 + 7 \times 10 \times 10 + 7 \times 10 = 1260$) of the Book of Revelation, and of some other monsters, such as the hydra and the number of seals.
- In the New Testament, the Gospel of Matthew 18:21, Jesus says to Peter to forgive 70 times seven times.
- There are seven suicides mentioned in the Bible.

Islam

- The ayat in surat al-Fatiha.
- The seven heavens in Islamic tradition.
- The seven Earths in Islamic tradition.
- The seven circumambulations (Tawaf) that are made around the Kaaba.
- The seven walks (Al-Safa and Al-Marwah); that is, traveling back and forth seven times during the ritual pilgrimages of Hajj and Umrah.
- The seven fires in hell; that is, the seven fires of hell.
- The seven doors to heaven, and hell is also seven.

staircase. Even Albert G. Mackey's *Encyclopaedia of Freemasonry* devotes two full pages to the number 7.

But why? Why is 7 so special that it elicits such significance?

One of the only possible explanations we could find relates to the original belief by ancients that there were seven planets. Early cultures considered the celestial bodies to be deities, and to these seven celestial bodies were given tremendous power and influence over the lives of humans on earth. Once additional planets were discovered, most cultures had already embedded the number 7 into their belief systems, and continued the legacy of lucky number 7,

Hinduism

- The Sanskrit word sapta refers to the number seven.
- The Indian music has sapta swaras, meaning seven octats (sa re ga ma pa dha ni), which are basics of music and are used in hundreds of Ragas.
- Celestial group of seven stars are named as Sapta Rishi based on the seven great saints.
- Seven Promises and Seven Rounds in Hindu weddings and Seven Reincarnations.
- As per Hindu mythology, there are seven worlds in the universe, seven seas in the world, and seven Rishies (seven gurus) called sapta rishis.

Mythology

- In Khasi mythology, there are seven divine women who were left behind on earth and became the ancestresses of all humankind.
- The number of gateways traversed by Inanna during her descent into the underworld.
- The number of sleeping men in the Christian myth of the "Seven Sleepers."
- The seven sages in Sumerian mythology and various other mythologies.
- The number of sages in Hindu mythology; their wives are the goddesses referred to as the "Seven Mothers."
- The number of main islands of mythological Atlantis.

infusing it into every area of life, including religion, myth, ritual, and celebration. Hieronimus and Cortner, in *The United Symbolism of America*, speculate that the number 7 got its good rap because it is a fundamental geometrical shape, one achieved by drawing a triangle around a square "which was done to symbolize the sky over

- In Guaraní mythology, the number of prominent legendary monsters.
- Japanese mythology talks of Shichifukujin (The Seven Gods of Fortune).

Others

- The minor symbol number of yang from the Taoist yin and yang.
- The number of palms in an Egyptian Sacred Cubit.
- The number of ranks in Mithraism.
- The number seven is of particular significance within Cherokee cosmology.
- In Buddhism, Buddha walked seven steps at his birth.
- In Irish mythology, the epic hero Cúchulainn is associated with the number 7. He has seven fingers on each hand, seven toes on each foot, and seven pupils in each eye. In the Irish epic Táin Bó Cúailnge, Cúchulainn is 7 years old when he receives his first weapons and defeats the armies of the Ulaidh. His son Connla is 7 years old when he is slain by Cúchulainn in "The Death of Aife's Only Son."
- In British folklore, every seven years the Fairy Queen pays a tithe to Hell (or possibly Hel) in the tale of Tam Lin.
- In the British folk tale of Thomas the Rhymer, he went to live in the faerie kingdom for seven years.

Courtesy of Wikipedia.

the earth, or by inscribing a triangle within a square, which was done to symbolize spirit within matter, the soul within man." They continue that 7 stands for "the complete period or cycle of time, such as seven days in a week, as well as the many other attributes previously mentioned."

23

Other numbers also hold unusual sway with humans, often appearing with frustrating frequency. One such example is the enigmatic number 23. It was the subject of a poorly received movie starring Jim Carrey, as a man plagued by the number. The "23 enigma" is the belief that all events revolve around the number 23, and that this number is implicated in every incident in a person's life in some form or another. But at least this time, we can trace the enigma to its source, namely several works of fiction via Robert Anton Wilson's *Illuminatus!* Trilogy and to William S. Burroughs (who first recounted his own involvement with the number in a story about a mysterious Captain Clark, whose ship and crew met with a terrible fate after 23 years, and the piloted flight #23 that was sent to find them). The number also plays a role in Discordian philosophy. Discordianism states that all events can be traced to the number 23 based upon the "ingenuity" of the interpreter. In other words, if you are clever enough, you can find a way to attach the number 23 to any significant event in your life. Imagine that—finally a number that we can all relate to! Does Kevin Bacon know about this?

The number 23 is certainly not alone. Take its closest relative for instance. The number 24.

666

We would be remiss in our duties if we did not explore one of the all-time most enigmatic numbers: 666. These three digits have long been the subject of great debate among religious scholars and amateurs alike. Again, we turn to the book of Revelation. In his vision on the Isle of Patmos, Saint John refers to a beast that bears the mysterious number 666. This is the alleged number of the

The 24 Enigma?

- There are 24 hours in a day.
- There are 24 ribs in the human body.
- 24 is the smallest number to have eight different factors. (1, 2, 3, 4, 6, 8, 12).
- 24 is the number of letters in both the modern and classical Greek alphabet. The 24th and last letter of the Greek alphabet is "Omega", meaning "the end."
- There are 24 "perfect" numbers. These are numbers that equal the sum of all its divisors except itself. (For instance, 6—the lowest of these numbers—is divisible by 1, 2, or 3, and 1 + 2 + 3 = 6.) The largest of the known "perfect" numbers has 12,003 digits.
- 24 is the largest number divisible by all numbers less than its square root.
- 24 is the number of cycles in the Chinese solar year.
- 24 is the number of books in the Tanakh.
- 24 is the total number of major and minor keys in Western tonal music, not counting enharmonic equivalents.
- The binary representation of 24 is 11,000.
- 24 is the sum of twin prime numbers (11 + 13).
- The earth travels 24,000 miles in 24 hours.

Antichrist that will wreak havoc upon the earth until the return of Jesus himself and the day of final judgment.

But why three 6s? If number 7 is considered the number of perfection, then the number 6 symbolizes that which falls short of perfection. One only has to recall the story of the fall of the angel Lucifer, because of his vanity and imperfection, to realize that the number 6, tripled, is empowered with negativity.

Beastly Number!

666 is an abundant number. It is the sum of the first 36 natural numbers (that is, 1 + 2 + 3 ... + 34 + 35 + 36 = 666), and thus a triangular number. Because 36 is both square and triangular, 666 is the sixth number of the form n2(n2 + 1) / 2 (triangular squares) and the eighth number of the form n(n + 1)(n2 + n + 2) / 8 (doubly triangular numbers).

666 is the sum of the squares of the first seven prime numbers. The harmonic mean of the decimal digits of 666 is an integer: 3/(1/6 + 1/6 + 1/6) = 6, making 666 the 54th number with this property. In base 10, 666 is a palindromic number, a repdigit, and a Smith number.

In the Eastern Orthodox Church, 666 is considered to be symbolic. Because 666 in Greek numerals stands for the Christ for man, because the man was created on the sixth day of Genesis, and the serpent represented what came between them.

The UPC barcodes found on most commercial products are characterized by guard bars at the beginning, middle, and end made

According to Wikipedia:

- In the Bible, 666 is the number of Adonikam's descendants who return to Jerusalem and Judah from the Babylonian exile.
- In the Bible, 666 is the number of gold talents that King Solomon collected in a single year.

up of two thin lines. Two thin lines also appear in the UPC encoding for the digit 6 (and no other digit), so to human eyes (but not to an electronic barcode reader) the guard bars appear to read 666. Some people interpret this as a fulfillment of the prophecy "Without this number an individual will not be able to buy or sell" (cited from the book of the Revelation 13:17).

The 2006 remake of the horror film The Omen *was released on June 6, 2006 (06/06/06) at 06:06:06 in the morning.*

The full name of former U.S. president Ronald Wilson Reagan contains six letters in each of his three names. This caused numerologists such as Gary D. Blevins to believe that Reagan was in fact the antichrist. Additionally, when Reagan moved to California following the end of his presidency, he asked that his house number be changed from 666 to 668.

In Chinese culture, 666 sounds a lot like the words meaning that things are going smoothly. It is considered one of the luckiest numbers in Chinese culture. It can be seen prominently in many shop windows across the country, and people there often pay extra to get a mobile phone number including this string of digits.

- The number 666 is a frequent visual element of Aryan Brotherhood tattoos.
- The sum of all the numbers on a roulette wheel is 666.

For some, the number 6 represents nothing more than man himself, with two arms, two legs, a torso, and a head. Six is also the trinity doubled.

Number anomalies abound. And you thought math was boring!

The number 37 will multiply into 111, 222, 333, 444, 555, 666, 777, 888, and 999.

3 x 37 = 111
6 x 37 = 222
9 x 37 = 333
12 x 37 = 444
15 x 37 = 555
18 x 37 = 666
21 x 37 = 777
24 x 37 = 888
27 x 37 = 999

If we are to label 666 as an "evil" number, then we must also ask the question: Was the original intention to be focused on the three digits themselves? Was it their sum of 18? Or, as in numerology, the sum of their sum—9?

Numeric anomalies exist everywhere, speaking of a higher intelligence adept at mathematical processing, one that often eludes us until we, well, crunch the numbers.

Because our lives are so intrinsically linked to numbers, we cannot avoid these synchronistic associations. And because we are humans, we then attach even further meaning to the synchronicity itself.

In the next chapter, we will learn about an actual "science," or maybe we should call it an "art" that uses numbers to predict the future and determine the fate of individual and collective destinies alike.

Is nothing random?

Chapter 6:6

NAME, RANK, AND SERIAL NUMBER

When you have mastered numbers, you will in fact no longer be reading numbers, anymore than you read words when reading books. You will be reading meanings.
—W. E. B. DuBois

God is ever a geometer. —Greek Pythagorean motto

There are those who believe that numbers have the power to shape our lives, our relationships, and our destinies. This belief is so prevalent that the study of numerology was established. Numerology consists of systems, traditions, or beliefs that posit a mystical or esoteric relationship between numbers and physical objects. Numerology and numerological divination were popular among early mathematicians, such as Pythagoras, but are now regarded as pseudomathematics by most modern scientists.

According to accepted scientific tenets, it would not be entirely accurate to call numerology a science. Rather, it can best be described as a belief system founded on the concept that the "number behind a name" can literally dictate a person's fate and fortune. Similar to astrology, numerology is based upon the idea that everything, even the names we were given by our parents at birth, has a profound meaning and purpose in the realization and unfoldment of our individual paths. From the jobs we choose to the places we live to the mates we give our hearts to, people throughout the centuries have studied their astrological and numerological charts and signs in hopes of gleaning prescient information that might enable them to make better informed life choices.

The study of numbers as a means of divination is believed by many historians to have its initial roots in Pythagorean mathematics. Once again, Pythagoras is a key player in the development of what we consider the merging of numbers and letters as a means of describing and determining character, motivation, and purpose. Though the actual roots are probably far older, for numerology does appear in the ancient Hebrew Kabbalah, it was the Pythagoreans who perfected the "art" to the point where it gained widespread acceptance as a method of divination, similar to astrology, which blends birth times and locations with celestial influences.

Other influences on the evolution of numerology come from early Christian mysticism, Gnosticism, and the Vedas, as well as from Chinese and Egyptian ancient esoteric traditions. St. Augustine of Hippo is quoted to have written, "Numbers are the Universal language offered by the deity to humans as confirmation of the truth" and he shared Pythagoras's conviction that numbers were behind everything in life. Obviously, after the Council of Nicea in 325 AD, the early Christian authority figures all but banned the practice as a form of "magic" and divination, along with astrology and other Pagan beliefs and traditions.

As the power of the Church rose to great heights during the Dark Ages, so too did the more shadowy "occult" traditions that were practiced by millions behind closed doors. This included the study of numerology, which further evolved as an esoteric "science" in just about every culture, including the Chinese, who created their own entire numerological system. Even the Tarot, passed down through the Middle Ages, was often associated with numerology. By matching the 22 major arcana to birth name letters and birth dates, the connection between numerology and tarot was understandably linked.

Moving ahead to the 1920s, it was most notably the work of fortune-teller Count Louis Hamon, writing as Cheiro, that truly popularized the art. Cheiro, author of *The Book of Numbers*, is responsible for the development of the "fadic" system of numbers. The fadic method added together all of the digits of a person's birth date to glean their final number of destiny. Books by L. Dow Balliett published in the early 1900s, and those in the 1930s by Florence Campbell, also served to revive this "pseudoscience" of number divination.

As a time of newfound enlightenment and spiritual discovery, the New Age movement of the late 1960s and early 1970s led to an increased awareness of numerology, combined with growing curiosity of such anomalies as time prompts, Y2K, 2012, the Bible Code, and other number-based mysteries. This interest seems to have vaulted this occult tradition into the mainstream. Talk to anyone nowadays, and chances are they know their "destiny number" or "summation number," the sum number of the letters of their birth name, which, as numerologists tell us, offers an intricate glimpse into our past, present, and future.

Though many of today's numerologists have expanded the basics into a whole range of potential readings, including birth name, life paths, destiny numbers, Soul Purpose numbers, Love Matches, and more, the most familiar way to use the numbers behind your personality is simply to take your full name given at birth, and find the corresponding digits, then add those for the total, or "summation number." But even that technique has variations. Let's use our names as an example:

The first technique simply adds up the digits in your name for the summation.

Marie Dauphine Savino—19 = 1 + 9 = 10 = 1 + 0 = 1. Marie is a 1.
Laurence William Flaxman—22 = 2 + 2 = 4. Larry is a 4.

The second technique gives a corresponding number to the letter according to its placement in the alphabet:

Marie Dauphine Savino	Laurence William Flaxman
M = 13	L = 12
A = 1	A = 1
R = 18	U = 21
I = 9	R = 18
E = 5	E = 5
D = 4	N = 14
A = 1	C = 3
U = 21	E = 5
P = 16	W = 23
H = 8	I = 9
I = 9	L = 12
N = 14	L = 12
E = 5	I = 9
S = 19	A = 1
A = 1	M = 13
V = 22	F = 6
I = 9	L = 12
N = 14	A = 1
O = 15	X = 24
	M = 13
	A = 1
	N = 14
Total: 204 = 2 + 4 = 6	Total: 229 = 2 + 2 + 9 = 13 = 1 + 3 = 4

Do It Yourself Numerology

Find the numbers that match your birth name letters and add them up to see what digit dominates your destiny.

A	1	H	8	O	15	V	22
B	2	I	9	P	16	W	23
C	3	J	10	Q	17	X	24
D	4	K	11	R	18	Y	25
E	5	L	12	S	19	Z	26
F	6	M	13	T	20		
G	7	N	14	U	21		

Thus, there would be a different final summation number for Marie, which means a different life path, purpose, and destiny depending on who would be doing her reading. Yet Larry's came out the same. Does that mean Marie has a split personality she knows nothing about?

Other techniques claim to utilize your common name, as in Marie D. Jones and Larry Flaxman. Others yet incorporate a host of other determining factors. For example, your full name at the time of reading, your confirmation name, nickname, or the name your spouse calls you when he or she is angry with you. Many modern numerologists also incorporate birth time and/or date into their readings.

Scientists see this wide range of potentials as part of the problem with taking numerology seriously. If there is no solid agreement as to which name, date, or birth time to use, how could anyone possibly be certain of the singular outcome of a reading as proof of destiny? It certainly does not lend credence to the art, or pseudoscience, of numerology, but, nonetheless, people swear by its outcomes, no matter how one gets to those outcomes.

BIRTH NAMES

The most widely used, oldest, and perhaps the most seriously studied forms of numerology use the birth name, for that is the name you were given at the moment of your entry into this life. As with astrology, which posits that the positioning of stars and planets influences our fate, numerology also posits that there is incredible influence on a person from the chosen name they are given. Perhaps the parents are infused with a subconscious inspiration that matches letter and number, and comes out simply as the urge to name one's child Jane, Elizabeth, Michael, or Gertrude. It might truly be an interesting exercise to examine some of the more unusual names, which are currently en vogue, and to see the patterns that emerge through time in chosen careers, love matches, and overall personality traits.

Once the Destiny Number, or Master Number as it is often referred to, is determined, there are variations on what personality traits—both positive and negative, one most associates with those numbers.

But all of this is according to the interpretation of those divining the numbers. In a sense, it is also open to the interpretation of the person receiving the reading itself. If you want to believe you are a powerful leader, having your number state you are "bold and obnoxious" could easily be interpreted as such. Ask anyone and they might claim those same positive and negative essences as a 1 or a 4, yet actually be a number 3, 5, or 8.

Ideally, a true numerological reading will get into much greater detail than what can be found on the many "do it yourself" websites or the introductory books that are in abundance in the New Age section of your local book store.

CHARACTER DESTINY

Similar to astrology, some readings result in a one-page summary of character and destiny, while there are others that result in a one hundred-page, highly detailed diatribe that literally maps a person's past, present, and future with stunning and inimitable accuracy. One has to wonder, though, if this is more a statement about the person doing the reading than the actual method of divination or interpretation.

Similar to our zodiac signs (with their helpful and harmful influences), or our Chinese Year signs (with their positive and negative traits), we seek to match who we are with when we came into the world, and what we were called when we got here. As a Libra and a Capricorn (Ox and Dog according to Chinese astrology), we have specific traits associated with our birth signs. Libras cannot make up their minds; Capricorns, thankfully, can. Libras are dreamy. Capricorns are more down to earth. Libras are outgoing. Capricorns are stable. The Ox is bold. The Dog is determined. The Ox is stubborn. The Dog is loyal. The Ox moves first, thinks later. The Dog thinks first, moves later. The Dog hikes his leg unsuspectingly ... okay, just kidding. We wanted to make sure you were still paying attention.

Many of these traits allow us to form beneficial relationships with others who have "compatible" numbers, signs, or symbols. Ox and Dog, although both highly competitive, make a powerhouse team. Yet again, many of the associated birth-sign traits could not be further from the truth about who we might really be. Perhaps it's a combination of nature and nurture when all is said and done.

FACT OR FICTION?

All over the world you will find many people living, loving, and working together who breach the code of "who goes together better," suggesting that perhaps these divination systems were meant to be more guideposts than full-on navigational systems one must follow to the last detail. The insightful website *Skepdic.com* points out on their numerology page, "When you get your reading, you may find yourself ignoring the parts that don't fit you at all, and focusing on those parts that do seem to fit. They may actually fit you or they may fit your image of how you would like to be." This is a critical aspect of any divinatory art: telling the client what they want to hear, even if the reader is motivated by sincerity of purpose. Throughout the ages, seers, prophets, psychics, and clairvoyants alike have similarly utilized this psychological trait to great effect—providing convincing readings and interpretations to those so eager for answers.

So, can numerology be simply attributed to a psychological "pat on the back"? Should we simply construe it as a recreational diversion—holding little to no validity? In our beliefs, no. Even Robert Todd Carol admits on his site *skepdic.com*, "Nevertheless, numerology shouldn't be brushed off without a thorough examination of its underlying theory." Granted, he goes on to say there does not seem to be any underlying theory to the skeptics, but those who know the true magic of numbers beg us all to look deeper.

There are several issues that scientists take against numerology, as well as every other divination method. The primary issue is the lack of cohesiveness to the system. Second, there are concerns regarding repeatability, empirical evidence, and often, sheer accuracy. There are so many different methods of calculating the matching numbers to letters: The English, Hebrew, Chaldean, Phonetic,

Chinese, Indian, and Pythagorean are a few that come to mind. If one uses the Chaldean method, the letter W equals 6. In the English system, it equals 5, the total of 2 + 3 (23rd letter). These are significant differences that could result in totally inaccurate readings. The disparity is such that someone could go home thinking that they are destined for show biz, when perhaps the truth is quite the opposite, and their real life path is in the mortuary business. Although, some might argue that there is little distinction between the two disciplines.

GEMATRIA

All humor aside, the art of numerology does have a foundation in esoteric knowledge; though, it goes back a long, long way.

One of the oldest references to the origin of numerology comes to us from the Hebrew Kabbalah. Known as "gematria," this Jewish mystical tradition associates numbers with letters from the Hebrew alphabet, then seeks hidden meaning in words that combine these letter/number forms. In gematria, entire words are converted into meaningful numeric associations; just as in numerology, a name is converted into a destiny or summation number by which divination occurs. But in gematria, similar words, with similar numeric values and contextual meanings are used to comment upon the original word, adding a richer depth to the system.

Ancient Greeks are said to have used the system of gematria to help interpret dreams, associating a numeric value to the letters of the Greek alphabet. Gnostics used the system to find hidden meaning behind the names of deities such as Mithra. Early Christians, most likely influenced by the Hebrew Bible, associated the numeric value of the Greek letters for alpha and omega, beginning and end, with the Greek word *peristera*, or dove (a symbol of Christ). That value is the number 801.

But it was the Kabbalists who developed gematria into a serious form of mystical knowledge, tradition, and divination, often utilized to seek the holy name of God, and to understand his ways and means via the numbers behind the words of their holiest of texts.

The word "gematria" comes from both Hebrew and Greek roots, with a link to the Greek word for geometry, and can be split into two traditions: "revealed" gematria, used in many forms of Rabbinic Judaism; and "mystical" gematria, more prevalent with those practicing Kabbalah. Gematria shares similarities with other numerological systems, namely the Greek version of isopsephy, numerology associated with the Latin language, and the Arabic Hisab al-Jummal. Some experts suggest gematria was first practiced by the Babylonian king Sargon II. In the eighth century BC, Sargon II may have even used the divination method to help construct the wall of Khorsabad, which was 16,283 cubits in length, the exact numerical value of his own name.

The most common gematria tradition is the revealed form, with roots in both the Talmud and Midrash, and has been written about by many commentators from later periods of time. This form focuses entirely on the power of assigning a numerical value to each letter of the Hebrew alphabet, with the end result being a word or combination of words that hold profound meaning, which were often said to be of a prophetic or divine nature.

The most widely studied tradition may be the mystical tradition that focuses on the 10 sefirot, or "fires of God," of the Kabbalistic tree of life, and the 22 letters of the alphabet. The mystical tradition, which further evolved more extensively in the writings of Zohar, also seeks to associate the letters of the alphabet with the 22 solids formed by regular polygons (five are Platonic solids, four Kepler-Poisot, and 13 are Archimedean). One solid was associated with one letter.

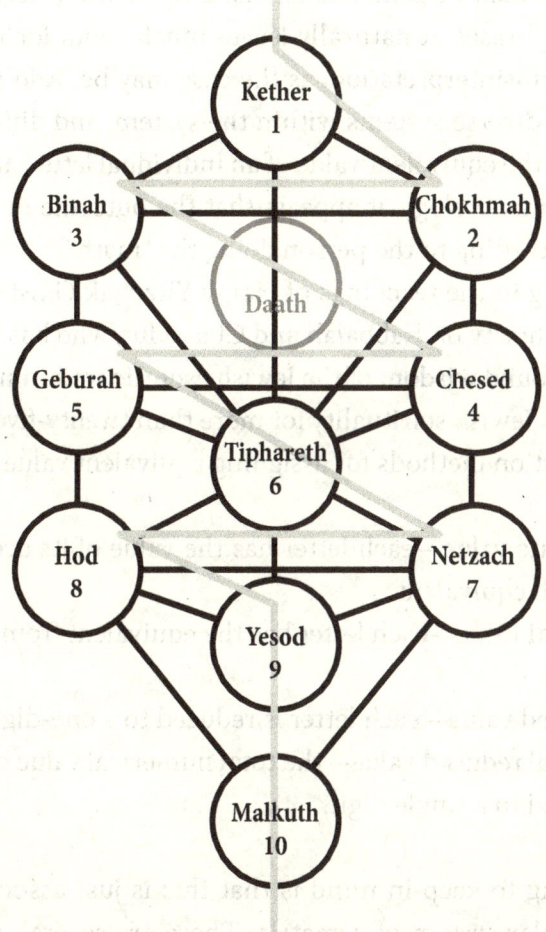

The Kabbalah Tree of Life corresponds the ten sefirot with letters of the Hebrew alphabet. Image courtesy of Wikipedia.

Thirteenth-century Kabbalists believed that there was a hidden code in the Old Testament, and that gematria could unlock the key that could read the code. This code was used to interpret whole verses by assigning numerical values to specific words. This practice was fine-tuned by the German scholar Eleazar of Worms, a commentarian writing during the same century.

Because much of gematria is based upon the interrelation of words and phrases, it naturally leaves much room for interpretation . . . or misinterpretation, as the case may be. Add to that the presence of diverse systems within the system, and different ways to calculate the equivalent value of an individual letter, and, similar to modern numerology, it appears that the outcome or end result can vary according to the person doing the "math."

According to the teachings of Harav Yitzchak Ginsburgh, a renowned authority on Kabbalah and Chassidut, who has been making the profound wisdom of the Jewish esoteric tradition accessible to seekers of Jewish spirituality for more than twenty-five years, the four calculation methods for assigning equivalent value are:

1. Absolute value—each letter has the value of its accepted numerical equivalent.
2. Ordinal value—each letter has the equivalent from 1 through 22.
3. Reduced value—each letter is reduced to a one-digit figure.
4. Integral reduced value—the total numerical value of a word is reduced to a single digit.

One thing to keep in mind is that this is just associated with one particular system of gematria. There are several, with other systems and sub-systems emphasizing varying decoding methods, such as the *notarikon*, which posits that the first letter of words can be combined to form new words; the opposite system, which takes the last letter of words to make new words or phrases; and the *temurah*, a complex system that organizes letters into tables that are then assigned specific mathematical values.

Even the early Christians felt the influence of the older Hebrew gematria. Theomatics, yet another numerology system, is based upon the Greek and Hebrew influences of the New Testament.

The term, coined in the 1970s by Del Washburn, coauthor (with Jerry Lucas) of *Theomatics: God's Best Kept Secret Revealed* and *Theomatics II : God's Best-Kept Secret Revealed*, is meant to bring together the words *mathematics* and *God*, and posits that God directly intervened in the writing of the Christian biblical texts. Basing itself on both Hebrew gematria and the Greek system of isopsephia, once again, a numerical value is given to each letter of both the ancient Hebrew and Greek alphabets, revealing distinct patterns that believers insist are not simply random or chance.

Ardent followers of theomatics claim that God himself placed the mathematical code into the biblical texts, and that each word of the Bible is spelled and placed into context with such intricate precision so as to literally document the entirety of past, present, and future. Names of people, names of locations, dates of events, and times of birth—were all orchestrated by this Divine Mathematician in an exact, predetermined location in the text to correspond with a numerical value meant for it and it alone. A Holy Magnum Opus.

RANDOM FACTS

W. Wynn Wescott, widely considered an extremely influential Satanist in the latter part of the 19th century, explains in his book, *Numbers: Their Occult Power and Mystic Virtues*:

> The followers of Pythagoras ... referred every object, planet, man, idea, and essence to some number or other, in a way which to most moderns must seem curious and mystical in the highest degree. "The numerals of Pythagoras," says Porphyry, who lived about 300 AD, "were hieroglyphic symbols, by means whereof he explained all ideas concerning the nature of things," and the same [numeric] method of explaining the secrets of nature is once again being insisted upon in

the new revelation of the *Secret Doctrine* by H.P. Blavatsky. "Numbers are a key to the ancient views of cosmogony—in its broad sense, spiritually as well as physically considered, to the evolution of the present human race; all systems of religious mysticism are based upon numerals. The sacredness of numbers begins with the Great First Cause, the One, and ends only with the nought or zero—symbol of the infinite and boundless universe.

Our innate desire for learning about, and gathering information related to our personal and collective destinies, won't go away anytime soon. Numbers have become such an integral part of our daily life that it is expected that we would attempt to look for meaning behind them as well. Sometimes that meaning comes in the form of synchronicities.

Chapter 7:7

SYNCHRONICITY

If the odds are a million to one against something occurring, chances are 50-50 that it will. —Anonymous

For those of us who grew up in the '80s, it would be hard to disagree that the bestselling Police album *Synchronicity* represents the feelings and emotions of the era quite well. Perhaps not surprisingly, Sting was a big fan of Carl Jung, the noted Swiss psychologist, and penned the song as a tribute to his theory of synchronicity. In fact, Sting was so enamored with Jung that the cover graphic of the album depicts him reading a copy of Jung's work! As he explained the theme of the song to *Time* magazine: "Jung believed there was a large pattern to life, that it wasn't just chaos. Our song 'Synchronicity II' is about two parallel events that aren't connected logically or causally, but symbolically."

The word *synchronicity* can be first attributed to Carl Jung, who used the word to describe the "temporally coincident occurrences of acausal events." Jung also used the terms "acausal connecting principle," "meaningful coincidence," and "acausal parallelism" to describe events that seemed to be much more than sheer coincidence. The concept of synchronicity did not escape such luminaries as Albert Einstein, who was fascinated by this principle of connectivity of events that could not, it seemed, be explained away by simple scientific means.

Jung stated that these synchronicities served to link the subjective world with the objective world. Hidden mathematical relationships between events speak of this link, as though beneath the structure of visible reality there exists a complex and detailed infrastructure, or, as we might say, "inner-structure." This implicate level of reality, to take a phrase from physicist David Bohm, may serve as a grid upon which all events occur, no matter their place in space or time, with some destined to occur simultaneously on several grid levels at a time.

Frank Joseph, former editor-in-chief of *Ancient American* magazine and author of several books on Atlantis, wrote in a *New Dawn Magazine* article titled "Synchronicity: The Key of Destiny" that numbers were one of many categories of synchronicity that people experience throughout their lives. He believed number synchronicities "thread together mystical human experience, often with surprising results."

Joseph, akin to many others, believes that when two events or objects share an association with the same number, there is more than mere coincidence behind the scenes. This is especially so when that number turns up repeatedly, as does 11:11 and other time prompts and sequences discussed throughout this book. If it happens once or twice, it might be a lucky coincidence, but seven, nine, or twelve times? And in one day? Now that is just too strange to be anything *but* on purpose.

Friedrich Schiller, the famed German poet and philosopher, is quoted as saying, "There is no such thing as chance; and what seems to us merest accident springs from the deepest source of destiny."

Noted French author Anatole France believed that "chance is perhaps the pseudonym of God when he does not wish to sign his work." This belief that synchronicities are signs or symbols originating from a higher power or being may be what forces us humans to give meaning to events occurring in unison. Meaning may not

Too Many 18s?

I was born on the 18th of May, 1962 (1 + 9 + 6 + 2 = 18). I was born at 9:54 a.m. (9 + 5 + 4 = 18). I was 18 inches long at birth. I was born in Louisville, Kentucky (Louisville has 10 letters and Kentucky has eight letters = 18 letters). I was officially adopted in the 18th month of my life (November 13, 1963). The number 18 is a 9-number in astrology, because 1 + 8 = 9. I turned 18 on May 18, 1980 (1 + 9 + 8 + 0 = 18). The last four digits of my Social Security Number add up to 18. My zip code ends with 18 (41018). At my job, I was originally hired as a shipper in the shipping department, and my shipper number given to me was 18. In 2000 our company installed a time clock for the first time, and my timecard barcode number adds up to 18. —Contributed by "Jim"

be necessarily implied in two number events colliding; rather, we imply the meaning to it. When this occurs, we marvel that, once again, we saw the number 876 nine times in one day, or had several run-ins with the number 62 in the last hour. Meaning is the element that we bring to a linked set of events the universe delivers to us.

Upon closer reflection, our lives always seem to follow some kind of pattern, or play out like a puzzle, with interlocking pieces. During Carl Jung's study and treatment of patients who had been diagnosed with emotional and mental disorders, he determined that there was an uncanny relationship between many patients' dreams and events that occurred in their waking life. One of the most famous and well-known cases involves a woman he treated who was difficult to break through. Jung listened intently as she described a strange dream involving a scarab beetle. At that very moment, one flew into the room and landed right before their eyes!

This is a rare insect, and not common to their geographic region. This experience was all that particular patient needed to see in order to liberate her from her mental blocks and begin the healing process.

It was almost as if some higher force knew she needed the validation.

Pareidolia and Apophenia

The human brain is hardwired to seek and find patterns wherever it can in order to understand a complex situation or arrangement. This is a primitive survival mechanism remaining from our prehistoric ancestors, when it was important to discern a stampeding boar from a pet goat in the dense underbrush. This phenomenon, known as "matrixing," or more commonly "pareidolia," is a universal human response. The term *pareidolia*, according to Wikipedia, describes a "psychological phenomenon involving a vague and random stimulus (often an image or sound) being perceived as significant. Common examples include images of animals or faces in clouds, the man in the moon, and hidden messages on records played in reverse." Are you a tea drinker? If so, have you ever attempted to "read" the leaves in the bottom of the cup?

The term *apophenia* means the ability of the human mind to seek and find meaning and significance where there seemingly is none. Klaus Konrad coined this term in 1958, and defined it as the "unmotivated seeing of connections" accompanied by a "specific experience of an abnormal meaningfulness." The terms *apophenia* and *pareidolia* are often used to explain unknown or paranormal events. More than likely you have experienced this at some point in your life.

According to Dr. Martina Belz-Merk, "There is currently a controversial debate concerning whether unusual experiences are symptoms of a mental disorder, if mental disorders are a consequence of such experiences, or if people with mental disorders are especially susceptible to or even looking for these experiences."

Skepdic.com has lengthy descriptions of both apophenia and pareidolia.

According to the site:

> The propensity to see connections between seemingly unrelated objects or ideas most closely links psychosis to creativity... apophenia and creativity may even be seen as two sides of the same coin. Some of the most creative people in the world, then, must be psychoanalysts and therapists who use projective tests like the Rorschach test or who see patterns of child abuse behind every emotional problem. Brugger notes that one analyst thought he had support for the penis envy theory because more females than males failed to return their pencils after a test. Another spent nine pages in a prestigious journal describing how sidewalk cracks are vaginas and feet are penises, and the old saw about not stepping on cracks is actually a warning to stay away from the female sex organ.
>
> Brugger's research indicates that high levels of dopamine affect the propensity to find meaning, patterns, and significance where there is none, and that this propensity is related to a tendency to believe in the paranormal.
>
> In statistics, apophenia is called a Type I error, seeing patterns where none, in fact, exist. It is highly probable that the apparent significance of many unusual experiences and phenomena are due to apophenia, e.g., ghosts and hauntings, EVP, numerology, the Bible code, anomalous cognition, ganzfeld "hits", most forms of divination, the prophecies of Nostradamus, remote viewing, and a host of other paranormal and supernatural experiences and phenomena.

The experience of apophenia is universal, and is experienced by many people throughout their lives. Skeptics argue that it seems highly likely that in the course of any long human life, linked events are bound to happen, and we, as humans, will find a way to label them as being relevant or important.

These same skeptics ask, how do we know the meaning we ascribe to them is the correct one? Is it personal, or a collective meaning from, as Jung believed, somewhere deep in the psyche ruled by archetype and symbol? Just because the meaning isn't obvious to the conscious mind, though, doesn't mean it isn't there. If most of our programming comes from the depths of the subconscious, it makes more sense that meaning arises from those same depths, and not from a place of analysis, judgment, and rational perspective.

If the 11:11 time prompts truly are a collective wake-up call, we have to entertain the notion that synchronicities happen on both an individual and collective level, with both individual and collective meanings. Because Jung believed that we access subconscious archetypes during these moments, we can postulate that there are number synchronicities that are meant to have meaning for the all as well as the individual.

Two people experiencing the same number event, or one person experiencing the same number or event throughout a specific time period, suggests not just a link of minds, but of ideas and perceptions. There appears to be an underlying pattern that is part of the entire framework, which again harkens back to the concept of an intricate, hidden layer of reality beneath that which we see, hear, touch, taste, and feel. During a lecture in 1951, Jung detailed his version of this larger framework, which was then published as *Synchronicity—An Acausal Connecting Principle* in a volume with related research by Nobel Prize winner Wolfgang Pauli.

Stories of Synchronicity:
A Journal Entry of a Dream

I was teaching art in a big, beautiful school, and my art room number was 11. I was called out of the room by a janitor dressed all in white, and he pointed to the hallway wall where the number 11 was printed next to the room number. He looked at me very meaningfully, as if to say, what will you do about it?

Immediately I began looking for the key to the room. The key was gold, but—I thought in my dream—a little cheap-looking, so I could give it to the substitute teacher. I had to go teach in a bigger school near Milwaukee, so I got in a small, round white vehicle that floated on an air cushion and was steered with a mouse-like device and took off down the highway.

This dream occurred just after I had left a job teaching art in Lake Geneva because of the very heavy schedule it entailed. After the dream, I began to see 11:11 everywhere... digital clocks, license plates, road signs, you name it, until it was driving me crazy. Finally I Googled it and to my surprise, found that there was actually a Website dedicated to the phenomenon. Ever since, the double-11s seem to come in clusters, and I always know something profound, big, or crazy is about to happen. When I see clusters of higher doubles, like 44-44, it seems to be more about spiritual things.

For me, it all ties into the idea of God's universe as a synchronous whole, and as an alert Intelligence that reaches out to communicate to those who have "ears to hear."

And as a postscript, I did end up getting another teaching job, at a smaller school, but it was located right next to a highway sign that read 11:11, on Hwy. 11, which I had to see every time I drove there.

—Linda S. Godfrey, *author of* Strange Wisconsin, The Beast of Bray Road, *and* Hunting the American Werewolf

TIME PROMPTS AND PHYSICS

Pauli, an Austrian-Swiss physicist, was intrigued by the links between physics and psychology, especially within the realm of quantum physics. He is noted for his work on spin theory, as well as for his discovery of the exclusion principle that links the structures of matter and chemistry. He also focused on the duality of the objective and subjective mind, with an emphasis on the impersonal nature of the objective mind. It was this mind that Jung suggested was the home of both the collective consciousness and collective archetypes, as well as the origin point of synchronistic experience.

Jung's fascination with symbol and archetype may have shaded his own personal interpretations of synchronistic events, but using the "keep it simple, stupid" (KISS) principle made famous by the tenet of Ockham's razor suggests that the simplest explanation is that these are, indeed, pure coincidence. Rather than attach all kinds of complex explanations to an experience, we look for the most simple, basic, fundamental cause—it just happened that way.

Medieval English philosopher and Franciscan monk William of Ockham (1285–1349) said, "Pluralitas non est ponenda sine necessitate." Translated, this means "Plurality should not be posited without necessity," and was a common principle in medieval philosophy. According to *Skepdic.com*, "Ockham's razor is also called the principle of parsimony. These days it is usually interpreted to mean something like 'the simpler the explanation, the better' or 'don't multiply hypotheses unnecessarily.' In any case, Ockham's razor is a principle that is frequently used outside of ontology, e.g., by philosophers of science in an effort to establish criteria for choosing from among theories with equal explanatory power. When giving explanatory reasons for something, don't posit more than is necessary."

Confirmation Bias

Random chance might lead to more connected experiences without an underlying meaning. What is referred to as "confirmation bias" is the likely culprit behind our resolute need to find or interpret information in a meaningful manner, all the while avoiding any evidence to the contrary. We believe what we want to believe, and hear and see what we want to hear and see, for personal reasons that often clash with what others believe, hear, and see. This is one of the main reasons for conflicts between religions and political parties (and in relationships, too!).

Pauli was critical of this confirmation bias theory, thus his support for Jung's work. Many scientists struggle with their need to explain away coincidences as meaningless, all the while trying to reconcile the fact that the evidence sometimes points to these occurrences as being too obvious to be *anything but* meaningless.

Cosmic Giggles

Nature indeed consists of patterns, as we've discussed previously, and perhaps more than anything, nature likes to pair things up. Terence McKenna, the prominent writer, philosopher, and ethnobotanist, referred to these events as "cosmic giggles," randomly moving "zones of synchronicity and statistical anomaly." McKenna's suggestion is that there may be a "science" to the synching of events, even if it appears utterly random while happening. For a great cosmic giggle it has long been suggested one listen to Pink Floyd's *Dark Side of the Moon* while watching *The Wizard of Oz*. Indeed, having done this a long, long time ago (Marie says, being of that particular era), the two seem to magically synch up. Whether this was intentional or a pure mystical coincidence, only the guys in Floyd know for sure. But this may be more a purposeful aligning of events than a random one, leading many people with way too much time on their hands to watch a host of old movies while listening to classic rock records, all in hopes of the next big "connection."

Time Prompts

People who experience time prompts and other synchronicities often refer to them as "miracles." Are they truly astonishing events, or are apophenia and pareidolia the explanation? Remember the KISS principle....

Cambridge University Professor J. E. Littlewood formed a new "law," known as Littlewood's Law, stating that the average individual can expect to experience one meaningful and significant event, that is, a miracle, each month. This law, which he described in more detail in his *A Mathematician's Miscellany*, sought to put the kibosh on the "supernatural" nature of such events. His rule is directly related to a theory that we will examine more closely in chapter 9:9, which basically suggests that if you take a large enough sample size of people, anything can (and usually does) happen!

Arguments aside, people are experiencing these linked events. They are ascribing meaning to them. And, in the case of popular numbers such as 11:11, they are assigning them a meaning ripe with collective significance.

Some people might view this as proof that our lives are predestined—set in stone and unchangeable. They view the occasional synchronicity as a reminder of that inevitability every now and then. Others see these unusual events as proof of the power of nothing more than cause and effect. One step leading to another... and not necessarily along a predetermined path.

But even the mere cause and effect theory begs the question: how are the causes and effects so intricately linked that each has such profound impact on the other?

Entanglement

Perhaps we need to examine the issue at the molecular or subatomic level. Could theoretical or quantum physics hold the key? Within quantum physics, the theory of entanglement suggests that particles that come in contact with one another remain "entangled" even over vast distances of time and space. Eerily, while not physically connected, they can have an instantaneous effect on the other. This "spooky action at a distance" freaked out the likes of Einstein, who died before it became acceptable as a fact. Entanglement all but guarantees that cause and effect is happening constantly and instantly, and, if on a more macrocosmic scale, showing up as the synchronistic experiences in our lives.

If, as physicist David Bohm states, reality is comprised of different levels—the explicate being the reality we see and experience; the implicate being the one we do not see underneath it all; and the super implicate being the sort of "godlike" reality that encompasses the other two—then what appears to be coincidence may simply be an event in one reality leaking over into the other. The same could be said for the theories of alternate dimensions and parallel universes, which are two popular concepts of theoretical and quantum physics now gaining momentum with mainstream science. An event occurring on Plane A in sequence with one occurring on Plane B would seem random, yet in the bigger scheme of things, there is nothing random about it at all. We may not see what goes on in Plane A, so we don't rationally make the connection that this was, indeed, a cause and effect event. Just because you don't see the initial cause doesn't mean that it isn't there . . . somewhere.

In her book, *The Rainbow and the Worm*, Dr. Mae Wan Ho suggests that some coherent nature of space and time may provide a framework for another type of reality. "A coherent space-time structure theoretically enables 'instantaneous communications to occur over a range of time scales and spatial extents.' What this implies in practice is a vast, unexplored area, as the notion of non-linear structured time this entails is alien to the conventional, western scientific framework."

Resonance

The idea of resonance also suggests that coherence of frequency, whether between two particles, different systems of the human body, or any other vibratory matter, can create the illusion, or quite possibly the reality, of phenomena that might be considered "paranormal." Two disparate events occurring simultaneously would fall into this theory of instant communication on a higher order of reality. Although the concept has been proven on a quantum level, it remains to be scientifically accepted on a grander scale.

Resonance may hold the key to a variety of unusual experiences, as we come to understand more and more about the role vibration plays in the makeup of matter and energy, as well as the way these things behave. The rate and intensity of vibrational frequencies of objects can create either harmony or discord between them, and perhaps it is when these frequencies complement each other, or synchronize, all matter of spooky action can occur, including paranormal events, psychic abilities, and strange coincidences that boggle the mind.

Symmetries

Once again, symmetries play a significant role in not just the fundamental nature of particles at the quantum level, but synchronicity, too. Werner Heisenberg, the "father" of quantum theory, believed that the most fundamental thing about nature was not necessarily particles, but particle symmetries.

In his book *Synchronicity: The Bridge Between Matter and Mind*, F. David Peat writes, "These symmetries could be thought of as the archetypes of all matter and the ground of material existence. The elementary particles themselves would simply be the material realizations of these underlying symmetries."

Heisenberg posited that these symmetries were the most fundamental level of our reality itself, something beyond mere photons and electrons, something that, as Peat words it, has "an immanent and formative role that is responsible for the exterior forms of nature." Peat goes on to ask, "Is it possible that archetypal symmetries of this nature could also manifest themselves in the internal structures of the mind?" What a great concept, in terms of how "without" can affect that which is "within" and vice versa, thus creating even more fertile ground for mysterious occurrences to take root.

Of course, the abstract natures of these symmetries have a mathematical aspect to them as they take place in "mathematically defined spaces." However, Peat points out, this is not necessarily an indication that particles "actually congregate together in space to form a pattern. Rather, it is their individual dynamic activity that, taken together, forms a pattern of mathematical transformations." And though we are talking about the dynamics of quantum matter, this same theory may apply to the manifestation of synchronicities in the macrocosmic world. Peat summarizes with this telling quote: "In this way it will be shown that there is no ultimate distinction between the mental and material so that synchronicities represent the explicit unfolding of deeper orders."

Because numbers are universal symbols, it makes sense that they should appear so often in synchronistic experiences. Again, from Peat, "It is only when certain aspects of the collective mind are projected into attention, clothed in the images and symbols of our particular culture, that we become aware of something universal that has come into the mind." This might explain the vast number of people who report thinking about an obscure, seldom-played song only to have it be played magically over the airwaves at just that instant.

Music, similar to math, is a collective language, an archetype we all operate from on a deeper implicate level. Finally, we close again with Peat, who said it so well: "Synchronicities are characterized by a unity of the universal with the particular that lies within a coincidence of events." The essence of this universal is seen in nature as patterns, symmetries, and even the laws of math that "interconnect a multiplicity of individual events." And indeed the possibility may exist that beneath this scientific framework lies a grid of creative and formative order that Peat calls "the objective intelligence."

Objective Intelligence

This objective intelligence is present throughout nature, permeating the known laws with a mysterious presence of something higher at work than mere functionality. Behind every structure there is an architect. Both the quantum and cosmic worlds posit the importance of the observer, as well as the conscious mind. In terms of synchronicities, we must also take into account the collective and objective mind that acts as a potential repository field from which our personal experiences rise. In this objective mind, the links between event A and event B are formulated, to be experienced by the subjective mind and given meaning to. Out of the chaos of nature, patterns emerge, and we glom onto those patterns and offer our own personally tailored interpretation. When they happen as often as time prompts do, the meaning becomes ever more important and profound.

In his book *The Synchronized Universe: New Science of the Paranormal*, physicist Claude Swanson, PhD, talks about the role of synchronicity on both the quantum and cosmic scale, and its relationship to the manifestation of paranormal. Though his massive tome refers more to psi, ghosts, and remote viewing, his theory of a reality made up of layers of universes makes for interesting mental fodder. Swanson posits that paranormal events can alter the structure of otherwise random or quantum noise, and thus alter the probability of events. Though we first need a more clearly defined understanding of the nature of this quantum noise, he notes that the potential exists to "extend current physics theory to understand and explain paranormal phenomenon." Swanson discusses the Zero Point Field (ZPF) as a possible state of fundamental quantum reality from which all matter, form, and energy springs forth. According to the Calphysics Institute:

> Quantum mechanics predicts the existence of what are usually called "zero-point" energies for the strong, the weak and the electromagnetic interactions, where "zero-point" refers to the energy of the system at temperature T=0, or the lowest quantized energy level of a quantum mechanical system . . . Zero-point energy is the energy that remains when all other energy is removed from a system.

This field of inquiry, championed by the work of physicist Hal Puthoff, one of the founders of the earliest university-backed remote viewing studies, could be the generative, formative field from which objective intelligence operates. That the universe itself is filled with fluctuating energy of random photons virtually popping in and out of existence suggests a potential hotbed of anomalous phenomena that might exist as well. The field of all potentiality, as Deepak Chopra referred to it, might contain within it all the information needed to create the synchronistic events we call coincidence. In addition, in this landscape of the field, where past, present, and future exist all at once, we might also find the origins of those strange, related experiences of déjà vu.

Swanson also cites resonance as a key to the synching of levels of reality. This synchronization would theoretically allow communication between levels, as well as create a Synchronized Universe Model (SUM). In summary, this SUM assumes that "all particles in the universe interact with one another," yet takes it a step further to posit that distant matter communicates with local electrons via the motion of photons, a connection that embodies the Mach Principle of distant matter determining local inertia and local forces. What does this have to do with seeing the number 10 fifty times in one day? Swanson believed the Mach Principle was a fundamental insight into the connectivity of reality, matter, and energy. Local forces having their origin in the distant matter of space.

Swanson's description of a layered reality of universes that, through resonance and coherence, could "synch up" and allow for the crossing of matter and energy, not to mention the possibility of paranormal phenomena, also suggests that the ability of events that seem to occur in different spatial and even temporal frames could "synch up" and create a miracle or coincidence. Thus, time prompts could be coming to us from different dimensions of space, as well as different dimensions of time.

Swanson refers to a single synchronized universe "represented by one sheet of paper in a stack. Each sheet has its own unique frequency and/or phase that characterize the synchronized motion of the electrons in that system. Other sheets represent 'parallel realities' or other 'parallel dimensions' that may cohabit the same space and time and yet be unaware of one another." But in the phase-locking of two or more "sheets," there is interaction of a synchronized manner. When the sheets are not in synch, no crosstalk occurs, and things appear as normal, even as random chance, with no connectivity to boggle the mind and startle the senses.

Consciousness, Swanson suggests, "interacts across these parallel dimensions. Thus it can affect and reduce the quantum noise. It can even synchronize motions between parallel realities. In this way higher forces (subtle energies) can be created, and energy can be extracted from these other dimensions."

When particles are in synch on their own "sheet," they obey the physical laws of that sheet. However, when they are in synch with those on a corresponding sheet, "the most dramatic paranormal effects are expected." It's an intriguing theory that does align with many concepts of both quantum and theoretical physics, and could also explain the ability of events to align and synch up at just the right place and time. If that is truly the case, then events may appear to have happened not at all by chance, but by some deeper design with deeper meaning. The mind or consciousness itself may even act similarly to this sheet system, with thoughts and interpretations moving between the objective intelligent state into the subjective, where significance is then either formulated or tossed aside. Again, information comes at us from all angles, even other layers of reality, but we choose which is important and what we pay attention to, based upon our survival needs. Yet every now and then, a thought or interpretation may slip through the veil of distraction and grab us by the collar, waking us up to the possibility that there is more to reality than meets the eye.

Chapter 8:8

JUST SIX NUMBERS?

God made the integers, all the rest is the work of man.
—Leopold Kronecker

Theories abound that the entire universe is based upon a very small and select group of numbers—mathematical equations that describe the whole of reality with intricate beauty and amazingly efficient detail. Physicists have long attempted to discover the magical Theory of Everything (TOE). This elusive theory will hopefully bring a seamless connection between the four fundamental forces of gravity, electromagnetism, and the strong and weak nuclear forces. Other theories regarding a universal framework also exist. One such theory is IT—Information Theory. IT is the concept of the universe as a computer, processing information in an increasing, compounding rate and spitting out new information to continuously expand what we see and experience as reality. Due to long-standing hesitance to change, scientists are only now beginning to openly discuss their belief in Information Theory.

But before we delve into Information Theory and attempt to show how the universe seemingly behaves like a computer processor, with "reality" actually being comprised of "its and bits" that shape and mold matter, we need to examine the importance of numbers in the creation of the universe itself.

SIX NUMBER THEORY

In his book *Just Six Numbers*, Sir Martin Rees, the Royal Society Research Professor at Cambridge University and Astronomer Royal, makes a bold case for explaining how just six fundamental numbers can explain the entirety of the physical cosmos. These numbers, "constant values that describe and define everything from the way atoms are held together to the amount of matter in our universe," were imprinted during the Big Bang itself and began a process of cosmic evolution that allowed for the creation of stars and galaxies, as well as all of the necessary energy states that govern matter and force as we know it. "Mathematical laws underpin the fabric of our universe—not just atoms, but galaxies, stars and people," Rees writes. "Science advances by discerning patterns and regularities in nature, so that more and more phenomena can be subsumed into general categories and laws." The goal of theorists, Rees continues, is to one day "encapsulate the essence of the physical laws in a unified set of equations."

Rees, as well as the growing number of researchers who have picked up on his work, believes that these mathematical values are so sensitive that if any of them were "untuned," there could be no stars and, therefore, no life—at least not life as we know and recognize it today. The reason these six numbers are so critical, Rees states, is because "two of them relate to the basic forces; two fix the size and overall 'texture' of our universe and determine whether it will continue forever; and two more fix the properties of space itself. . . ." Different choices of the six fundamental numbers, Rees tells us, would give us a much different universe . . . maybe even a sterile one.

The six fundamental numbers that shape the universe, and helped make it in the first place, are:

Just Six Numbers?

1. **Nu—"N," a critically huge number with the value of 1,000,000,000,000,000,000,000,000,000,000,000,000,000**. This is a ratio of the strength of electrical forces holding atoms together, divided by the force of gravity (which is 10 to the 37th power) between them. If this number were smaller, even by a few zeros, it has been posted that the universe's lifespan would be too short for biological evolution to occur. As Rees states, a short-lived universe would mean that no creatures could ever grow larger than insects, with no time for biological evolution to unfold. Thus, a buggy world indeed.

2. **Epsilon—0.007.** Another ratio, this time the proportion of energy released when hydrogen fuses into helium. This number defines how firmly atomic nuclei bind together and how all of the atoms on earth were made. The value of epsilon controls the power from the sun and how stars transmute hydrogen into all the atoms of the periodic table. Carbon and oxygen are common, and gold and uranium are rare, because of what happens in the stars. Were this number 0.006, or 0.008, Rees states that we could not possibly exist, again suggesting that the smallest tweaks would have resulted in a universe far different from this one.

3. **Omega—The cosmic number 1** measures the amount of material in our universe—galaxies, diffuse gas, and dark matter. Omega refers to the relative importance of gravity and expansion energy in the universe. According to Rees, a universe with too high of an Omega level would have collapsed long ago; too low, no galaxies would have formed. The inflationary theory of the Big Bang says omega should be one, but astronomers have yet to measure its exact value. Some scientists point to the finely tuned initial speed of expansion as a hint of Creative Intelligence.

4. **Lambda**—The force of cosmic antigravity that was discovered in 1998. This is an extremely small number and appears to control the expansion of the universe; however, it has no effect on scales of less than a billion light years. If lambda were any larger, its effect would have stopped galaxies and stars from forming, and cosmic evolution would have been "stifled before it could even begin."
5. **Q = 1/100,000**—The basic seeds for all cosmic structures such as stars, galaxies, and clusters of galaxies, all of which were imprinted in the Big Bang itself. The fabric—or texture—of our universe depends on a number that represents the ratio of two fundamental energies. If Q were smaller, the universe would be inert and without structure; if Q were much larger, the universe would be a violent place where no stars or suns could exist, dominated by giant black holes.
6. **Delta—3.** The number of spatial dimensions in our world. Rees argues that life can only exist in three dimensions, not two or four. This number, it seems, has been known for hundreds of years, but is now being viewed in a whole new way, especially in light of superstring theory, which posits that the most fundamental underlying structure are vibrating superstrings that operate in a potentially ten-dimensional "arena."

So far, Rees and his colleagues have been unable to find the one great undeniable link between all these numbers that would result in a mathematical Theory of Everything (TOE), if one such theory exists, but these fundamental ratios and numbers do build one upon the next to create a sort of cosmic blueprint. These "pieces of a puzzle" may possibly be used to describe the nature of the universe and its forces, and certainly speak to the idea that beneath it all there is a grand plan or design that works. We humans are proof of that.

Just How Finely Tuned Is the Universe?

It is quite spooky to think that with some minor tweaks here and there, we would not exist. These are just some of the reasons why....

If the strong nuclear force constant was larger: no hydrogen would form; atomic nuclei for most life-essential elements would be unstable; thus, no life. If smaller: no elements heavier than hydrogen would form; again, no life.

If the weak nuclear force constant was larger: too much hydrogen would convert to helium in big bang; stars would convert too much matter into heavy elements making life impossible. If smaller: too little helium would be produced and stars would convert too little matter into heavy elements, making life impossible.

If the gravitational force constant was larger: stars would be too hot and would burn too rapidly and too unevenly for life chemistry. If smaller: stars would be too cool to ignite nuclear fusion; thus, many of the elements needed for life chemistry would never form.

If the ratio of electromagnetic force constant to gravitational force constant was larger: all stars would be at least 40 percent more massive than the sun; stellar burning would be too brief and too uneven for life. If smaller: stars would be at least 20 percent less massive than sun and incapable of producing heavy elements.

If the ratio of electron to proton mass was larger: chemical bonding would be insufficient for life. If smaller: same as above.

If the ratio of number of protons to number of electrons was larger: electromagnetism would dominate gravity, preventing galaxy, star, and planet formation. If smaller: same as the previous reason.

If the expansion rate of the universe was larger: no galaxies would form. If smaller: the universe would collapse, even before stars formed

Adapted from Hugh Ross, PhD, The Creator and the Cosmos

Reasons for the Universe

In Rees's opinion, there are three explanations for the finely tuned universe in which we seem to live, one that is dependent upon the previously discussed six numbers. First, we must consider sheer coincidence. It is certainly a possibility that we are here just because that's the way the numbers were tuned with no deeper meaning attached. Second, many scientists suggest that the specific tuning of these six numbers, so intricately perfect, lends itself to the argument in favor of a Creator—or "intelligent design." This theory is gaining ground with reputable scientists as a viable alternative to the long-standing belief in evolutionism. According to the official website of ID (*intelligentdesign.org*):

> Intelligent design refers to a scientific research program as well as a community of scientists, philosophers and other scholars who seek evidence of design in nature. The theory of intelligent design holds that certain features of the universe and of living things are best explained by an intelligent cause, not an undirected process such as natural selection. Through the study and analysis of a system's components, a design theorist is able to determine whether various natural structures are the product of chance, natural law, intelligent design, or some combination thereof. Such research is conducted by observing the types of information produced when intelligent agents act. Scientists then seek to find objects [that] have those same types of informational properties [that] we commonly know come from intelligence. Intelligent design has applied these scientific methods to detect design in irreducibly complex biological structures, the complex and specified information content in DNA, the life-sustaining

physical architecture of the universe, and the geologically rapid origin of biological diversity in the fossil record during the Cambrian explosion approximately 530 million years ago.

At the very least, this Creator wanted us humans to show up, and tuned the universe with that specific intention in mind. "If you imagine setting up the universe by adjusting six dials, then the tuning must be precise in order to yield a universe that could harbor life," Rees states. The question is: who or what is responsible for the tuning? (See chapter 10:10 for more on this!)

Last, but certainly not least, is the idea that we are not alone in terms of being the only universe to have experienced a Big Bang. Other universes may exist, each with their own rate of cooling, their own fine-tuning, and their own laws, which are defined in the end by a different set of numbers. As Rees puts it, "This may not seem an 'economical' hypothesis—indeed, nothing might seem more extravagant than invoking multiple universes—but it is a natural deduction from some (albeit speculative) theories, and opens up a new vision of our universe as just one 'atom' selected from an infinite multiverse."

The intricate omega, for example, which simply describes the density of the universe, is so precise that, as a result, we are all able to exist. It's confounding to think that were this value just a tiny bit higher, our infant universe might not have begun expanding, and gravitational forces would have run amok, causing what some describe as a "great crunch" instead of a "big bang." And if the amount of mass present was any lower, gravity would never have had a chance to allow particles to connect and interact, forming into objects, and ultimately life. Were these tunings just the result of the way matter and energy blew apart during the Big Bang itself? Was this intricacy coded somehow into the pre-Bang singularity from which the universe was formed? When was the plan written . . . and by whom or what? Let's look at "N."

N

"N" dictates how big the universe is allowed to get, and beyond that or below that value, the gravitational force might exceed the electric force, and the universe would not exist. Were gravity significantly stronger than we know it, our reality might be very different, and we would likely be seeing a lot more black holes around us. Definitely not a good thing! The relationship between electromagnetism and gravity is, again, so finely tuned as to allow for things to be just as they are, from the smallest to the largest objects, governed by laws that keep things in a cohesive state. One minor tweak, and it would be utter chaos.

Each of these six fundamental numbers would seem to be utterly critical to the absolute "rightness" of the universe that we live in, a rightness that allowed for all the perfect combinations, events, and interactions to lead to life, at least on our little planet. According to *Is God a Mathematician* by Mario Livio, English astronomer James Jeans said, "The universe appears to have been designed by a pure mathematician." The laws that govern motion, gravitation, force, and matter are all, at their foundation, mathematical laws that give order to nature and form the bedrock of all physical reality. The word *astronomy* itself means "law of the stars," and those laws have their basis in mathematics. Even the esteemed 13th-century scholar Roger Bacon recognized that natural laws were fundamentally mathematical laws. According to the classic *Encyclopedia Brittanica*, Bacon's *Opus Majus* states:

> "Part IV" (pp. 57–255) contains an elaborate treatise on mathematics, "the alphabet of philosophy," maintaining that all the sciences rest ultimately on mathematics, and progress

only when their facts can be subsumed under mathematical principles. This fruitful thought he illustrates by showing how geometry is applied to the action of natural bodies, and demonstrating by geometrical figures certain laws of physical forces. He also shows how his method may be used to determine some curious and long-discussed problems, such as the light of the stars, the ebb and flow of the tide, the motion of the balance. He then proceeds to adduce elaborate and sometimes slightly grotesque reasons tending to prove that mathematical knowledge is essential in theology, and closes this section of his work with two comprehensive sketches of geography and astronomy. That on geography is particularly good, and is interesting as having been read by Columbus, who lighted on it in Petrus de Alliaco's Imago Mundi, and was strongly influenced by its reasoning.

In his book *The Goldilocks Enigma: Why Is the Universe Just Right for Life?* author and physicist Paul Davies states, "The ancients were right: beneath the surface complexity of nature lies a hidden subtext, written in a subtle mathematical code. This cosmic code contains the secret rules on which the universe runs." Davies, also the author of *The Mind of God*, reminds us that early scientists such as Galileo and Newton believed that by exposing the patterns behind the fabric of nature, they could somehow get a glimpse of the mind of God. This religious quest parallels the more modern belief by today's scientists, many of them by no means religious, where Davies says that "an intelligible script underlies the workings of nature, for to believe otherwise would undermine the very motivation for doing research, which is to uncover something meaningful about the world that we don't already know."

Davies believes that science has indeed "uncovered the existence of this concealed mathematical domain." We humans, he goes on, have been made "privy to the deepest workings of the universe," and, unlike the animals who simply observe these workings, we humans alone have the power to try to explain them.

Many theories and explanations regarding the nature of the universe exist, and like the turtle theory in the sidebar, there must be what is called the "termination of the chain of explanation." To explain a theory, there must be a beginning and an end. A start and a finish. The woman at this lecture apparently felt that a bottomless chain of turtles was a perfectly rational and reasonable explanation, or perhaps, as Paul Davies suggests in *The Goldilocks Enigma*, there is a levitating super-turtle upon which the chain of turtles stands. Of course, we can laugh at this concept, but it illustrates the difficulties that come along with theorizing anything about the nature of reality itself! Perhaps the joke is on us.

THIS UNIVERSE . . . AND BEYOND!

As we continue to make further advancements into the study of cosmology, and our ability to see into the heart of deep space improves, other ratios and numbers may be added to complete the architectural framework of the cosmos. These six initial and fundamental numbers also may provide for the possibility of multi-dimensional strings and parallel universes. Rees himself is a proponent of the multiverse theory, and the idea is growing in popularity among theoretical and quantum physicists. According to an article by Aurelien Barrau in the *International Journal of High-Energy Physics*, "The idea of multiple universes is more than a fantastic invention. It appears naturally within several theories, and deserves to be taken seriously." Barrau further states: "This multiverse—if true—would force a profound change of our deep understanding of physics. The laws reappear as kinds of phenomena; the ontological primer of our Universe would have to be

Numbers or Turtles?

There is a story often attributed to both Bertrand Russell and to the 19th-century American philosopher William James. The story revolves around a lecture being given about the nature of the universe. Halfway through the lecture, a woman stands up in the back of the room and denounces the lecturer, proudly claiming that she knows the exact nature of how the universe is put together. Her claim? That the Earth rests on the back of a giant elephant that is, in turn, standing on the back of a giant turtle. Stunned, the lecturer asks her what the turtle is standing upon. The woman shouts back, "You must be a very clever young man, but you can't fool me! It's turtles all the way down!"

abandoned. At other places in the multiverse, there would be other laws, other constants, other numbers of dimensions; our world would be just a tiny sample. It could be, following Copernicus, Darwin, and Freud, the fourth narcissistic injury."

In fact, quite simply, different universes would have formed at different rates, cooled at different rates, and therefore be governed by different laws, numbers, and ratios from our own. Thus, our Big Bang could have been one of many (part of M-theory) that was created with its own specific set of mathematical components at the core of its expansion and evolution. In our universe, these six cosmic numbers are the only things that keep us from being one of those badly tuned universes where nothing expands, forms, coheres.... Talk about being in the right place at the right time! The subatomic forces that shape and mold our very reality exist because of such a honed, perfected tuning of the rate of expansion after the

Big Bang. The sensitivity to these six numbers seems apparent in the physical laws that governed the processes behind the formation of galaxies, stars, and planetary systems.

Undoubtedly, this raises more questions than answers. The biggest questions the mathematical nature of order begs are: Can there then be an "intelligence" behind these numbers? Is this a stable system, and is there room for such concepts as entropy, disorder, and chaos? The idea that these numbers are attuned, and create a potential formula that links them together, then begs the question: Who or what "attuned" them? The mathematical formulas behind all six values are so perfectly deliberate one would think that the creative force of the entirety of reality was a gigantic calculator . . . or perhaps a computer. We will first look at the concept of the universe as a computer, which again will ask those pesky questions: Who is the Master Programmer? Who developed the initial language?

The Universe as a Computer

The question on the lips of many cutting-edge mathematicians, cosmologists, astronomers, and physicists is:

Could the universe simply be a massive quantum computer?

In order to explain the vast complexities of our universe, many scientists look to the technology age as a guide to just what might account for the sheer volume of "stuff" that fills our world. The basis of this theory starts with the idea that particles and their interactions are not solely responsible for transferring energy but information as well. Bits of information.

Bits and bits.

"The universe is the biggest thing there is and the bit is the smallest possible chunk of information. The universe is made of bits. Every molecule, atom, and elementary particle registers bits of information. Every interaction between those pieces of the universe processes that information by altering those bits . . . the universe is a quantum computer," writes Professor Seth Lloyd in *Programming the Universe: A Quantum Computer Scientist Takes on the Cosmos*. In an interview with the Edge Foundation, Professor Lloyd states:

> It's been known for more than a hundred years, ever since Maxwell, that all physical systems register and process information. For instance, this little inchworm right here has something on the order of Avogadro's number of atoms. And dividing by Boltzmann's concept, its entropy is on the order of Avogadro's number of bits. This means that it would take about Avogadro's number of bits to describe that little guy and how every atom and molecule is jiggling around in his body in full detail. Every physical system registers information, and just by evolving in time, by doing its thing, it changes that information, transforms that information, or, if you like, processes that information.

Is it possible that, like a giant information processing system, the universe computed itself into existence via the Big Bang? Once this initial computation is complete, perhaps it then compounds the amount of initially programmed information with newly computed information . . . then "it" begins the task of processing it all over again in a cyclical pattern. The result is a snowball effect of continuously created "stuff," the variety of which is ever-increasing, ever-expanding.

The formation of atoms and other elementary particles, then, would consist of specific amounts of information in the form of its and bits, and as the universe processes this information to create more particles and matter, it also corresponds to the laws of physics, chemistry, and biology—all of our known laws that govern structural behavior and other physical elements. Similar to a huge computational system, the universe appears to some to have a "scripted quality" that suggests, as Seth Lloyd states, "the same astral dramas are played out again and again by different stellar actors in different places."

In a computational universe system, entropy acts as the "information required to specify the random motions of atoms and molecules." These motions are too small to be seen or measured, so Lloyd posits that entropy can also be described as that information in a physical system that we cannot see—one that remains outside our visible awareness. Entropy also determines the amount of thermal energy in a system that has usefulness. Entropy is an integral part of the second law of thermodynamics, which states that the entropy of the universe does not decrease as a whole, but rather the amount of unusable energy increases. One way to think about the concept of entropy is to picture it corresponding in quantity to the number of bits required to describe or quantify the jiggle of atoms. Heat itself is the energy behind the jiggle; entropy describes the information behind the jiggle.

As a giant computer, the its and bits of information that are required to process anything and everything into existence that we can see—that is, a planet—prove staggering in number. But even the materials required to form an electron requires a staggeringly large number of pieces of information, again, most of which remains beyond our visibility. "Ultimately," Lloyd writes, "information and energy play complementary roles in the universe: Energy makes physical systems do things. Information tells them what to do."

This interplay between the physical and the informative, physics and information, is the dance of the "computational nature" of the universe itself. In the mid-20th century, such notable scientists as Harry Nyquist, Claude Shannon, Norbert Wiener, and their colleagues devised and formulated the theory behind the mathematical nature of this interplay with the utilization of mathematical arguments to create actual amounts of information that would be required to do specific things. An example of this would be in the number of bits required to send a communication down a telephone line. These researchers formulated what is now "Information Theory," which was later refined by James Clerk Maxwell and Ludwig Boltzmann.

In an interview with Jason Cosmowiki of *Strange Ideas*, Seth Lloyd described the universe as "one big honking quantum mechanical computer," suggesting that the universe itself is simply a simulation. A representation that is so exact that one could not distinguish it from reality. Although this sounds very "Matrix-esque," the idea that the universe acts as a quantum computer suggests that decoherence is the key to what we then see as reality. When quantum bits decohere, or choose one path over another in the processing progression, specific structures arise and form. According to adherents of the quantum universal model, this is what gives the universe the appearance of being "programmed." The suggestion is that specific choices are made within the system as they would be in a computer, where certain its and bits of information are utilized above others, with the end result being what we see and perceive as everything from atoms to black holes. Different choices suggest a different universe.

In his book *Decoding the Universe: How the New Science of Information Is Explaining Everything in the Cosmos, from Our Brains to Black Holes* (which wins the grand prize for world's longest book title!), author Charles Seife examines this concept of a Cosmic Computer. Seife, like a growing number of researchers, believes that this computer has programmed itself and all of reality into existence. Pretty heady stuff!

Seife looks at Information Theory as a way to possibly understand the odd principles at play in the universe by focusing on the physicality of information. Information, he suggests, is a "concrete property of matter and energy which is quantifiable and measurable."

Yet this information is subject to physical laws, and these laws, as in any other area of natural science, do dictate the behavior of mass and energy as information.

All of this information has to be transmitted and communicated, and this process of transmitting its and bits through space uses energy, all of which is measurable and precisely programmed to deliver a specific coded set of information that will eventually be a planet or star. The universe, thus, could indeed be the fastest and most efficient computer ever dreamt of by those who follow Moore's Law. Moore's Law was created in 1965 by Gordon Moore, cofounder of Intel, and states that the total number of transistors per square inch on integrated circuits (IC) had doubled every year since the IC was invented. As a measurement of computing power, Moore's Law basically states that computing power doubles roughly every two years. Imagine the amount of computing power within the universal computational system doubling at such a rate! The sheer volume of information would be staggering, snowballing into more information with farther reaching capabilities. It's truly astounding to think of the potential power and speed of this system.

But again, all of this begs the question, who or what is doing the programming?

And going back to the multiverse theory, one might also ask, does each universe have its own program/programmer, or is there a Master Program/Programmer behind the curtain, as in Oz? These are the challenges of Information Theory's leading proponents, who seek to comprehend and understand the power of the its and bits.

Pi

Six numbers and its and bits aside, there is another number that seems to speak of a nature far more profound than its quantitative value. Pi, or 3.14, is nothing more than the ratio of the circumference of a circle to its diameter. Pi is the 16th letter of the Greek alphabet. In the system of Greek numerals it has a value of 80.

Based on the Greek word *periferia*, meaning "circumference," and represented by the Greek letter *p*, this simple irrational number has origins so ancient that some scholars say they may be untraceable to the source. Pi is not only an irrational number, meaning that it is unable to be expressed as a ratio of two different integers and that its decimal expression never ends and never starts recurring, but it is also what is known as a "transcendental number." These numbers are described by Wikipedia as "a complex number that is not algebraic; that is, not a solution of a non-zero polynomial equation with rational coefficients. In other words, transcendental numbers are numbers that do not arise from ordinary algebraic expressions."

The symbols for pi are universal, as is the meaning behind the symbols.

Although Pi is certainly an interesting number, its mystique likely comes from the fact that it is one of the oldest mathematical quantities that we can trace throughout history. Some scholars attribute Archimedes with the first real theoretical work involving pi, with other mathematicians adding to the growing body of understanding of this simple number throughout the ages. One of the most fascinating aspects of pi is its ability to calculate the circumference of a circle around massively large spheres. This computation can be performed to a very high degree of accuracy thanks to its infinite decimal expansion.

Pi is one of those unusual numbers, as are omega, delta, and the others about which Sir Martin Rees writes that would no doubt be the same for an alien from another universe. It represents a relationship, a ratio that is always going to be the same value, no matter what universe you are in, and no matter the size of the object of measurement. Pi is pi no matter where you go. This type of constant is literally a part of the fabric of our universe, and perhaps many others as well.

Pi has a reputation as being somewhat of a "controversial" number, with several alternate interpretations being hypothesized. According to Michael Hayes, author of *The Hermetic Code in DNA: The Sacred Principles in the Ordering of the Universe*, pi is associated with music, harmonics, and DNA itself. The "mathematical convention pi," as he refers to it, corresponds with the numerals 22/7, a symbol of the "triple octave," and a formula fully known about by ancient Egyptians, who incorporated it into their daily activities, as well as with the building of the pyramids. This same relationship is also apparent in the pyramid structures of Teotihuacán, Mexico, and, as Hayes states, even England's Stonehenge. Does this sound suspiciously like a sacred number?

Pi's musical association is, according to Hayes, "designed to express the law of seven and the law of three—the triple octave, composed of 22 notes." Each of the three individual octaves is also composed of three "inner" octaves, Hayes proposes, totaling nine octaves and "exactly 64 fundamental notes, the square of the constant number 8." Hayes calls this the "Hermetic Code," and states it is a universal formula found everywhere, including the structure of our own DNA.

The "mathematical" pi has a value closer to 3.14159. The "classical" pi value is 3.142857. . . . Regardless, the universal symmetry Hayes and other researchers have found between pi and the fundamentals of harmonics also seems present in the structure of the genetic code, which we will discuss further in chapter 10:10. Hayes states, "The Hermetic Code, as we know, is primarily an expression of the law of triple creation, which holds that everything is composed of trinities within trinities. This means that the three individual octaves embodied within pi are in themselves triple octaves, making nine octaves in total, or sixty-four notes—precisely the number of RNA codon combinations."

This has very far-reaching implications, and as Hayes writes:

> Where this conclusion leaves us, the human race, we can but speculate, but the fact that the genetic code of the microcosmic world of the cell, and the hermetic code in the macrocosmic world of the human mind are absolutely identical is surely significant. It, in fact, brings to mind the principal dictum of Hermes Trismegistus, which was inscribed on the legendary Emerald Tablet: "As above, so below."

The implication one immediately draws from this is that the only difference between the DNA helix and a fully functional human brain is simply one of scale. And if the human brain is a kind of metaphysical "helix," then presumably it is also an integral component—a cell-nucleus—in the body of an infinitely greater, multidimensional "organism"—our own galaxy, perhaps.

Pi's magnificence suggests again that behind all of what we see and don't see, there is a structured measurement with mathematical principles. The very fabric, and foundation, of our existence, and how we measure the world of reality around us, is entirely dependent on numbers. Yet, this dependency hints strongly that there is a force behind the math of such vast and precise intelligence and order.

Chapter 9:9

THE TROUBLE WITH NUMBERS

The last function of reason is to recognize that there are an infinity of things which surpass it. —Blaise Pascal

As we have seen in the preceding chapters, numbers and mathematical modalities play an integral role in virtually all aspects of our existence. Mathematical law may even serve as the foundation for all of reality. The universe could probably be described within the confines of just six numbers. The laws of physics might actually be the laws of the land. Wouldn't the seeming simplicity of that concept be a refreshing change from our complex and busied existence? If we could take numbers and their properties at face value, life might be so much less ... well ... intricate.

But that suggestion doesn't necessarily mean that numbers are always the magical, mystical, and mysterious miracles that we imagine them to be. Any good writer, or writing team, in this case, worth its weight in gold would be remiss to pass up the chance to play devil's advocate and present the opposing viewpoint. Even when it comes to numbers and the profound mystique they suggest, we have to understand that there are other laws that take the complex and swap it for the simple. Remember our friend William of Ockham and his principle of Ockham's razor? With all other things being equal, generally the simplest possible explanation is the correct one.

Many of the more mundane laws involving numbers were discovered out of the sheer curiosity of mathematicians and scientists who were simply not satisfied with the "magical" properties ascribed to specific patterns and rates of frequency that were uncovered during their research.

PASCAL'S TRIANGLE

Consider Pascal's Triangle. This is a geometric arrangement of digits that describe the "binomial coefficients" in a triangle. In plain English, that means that "in mathematics, the binomial coefficient is the coefficient of the xk term in the polynomial expansion of the binomial power $(1 + x)$ n. In combinatorics, it is often called the choose function of n and k; it is the number of k-element subsets (the k-combinations) of an n-element set; that is, the number of ways that k things can be 'chosen' from a set of n things." That description, from Wikipedia, would take a textbook to explain, but our interest in Pascal's Triangle goes far beyond what it helps determine the value of.

This intriguing Triangle was named after Blaise Pascal, who first wrote about his use of the Triangle to solve problems in probability theory back in 1655. But the Triangle had been studied and written about much earlier, even as far back as the 10th century in commentaries written about the ancient Sanskrit *Chandas Shastra*. This work initially dates the use of the Triangle back to the 5th century BC, with the Indian mathematician Bhattotpala later expanding upon the rows of the Triangle. Persian mathematician Al-Karaji and astronomer-mathematician Omar Khayyam further expounded upon the Triangle between 953 and 1131 AD, thus the added name of "Khayyam's Triangle."

Thanks to mathematician Yang Hui in the 13th century, the Chinese had their own version, today known as "Yang Hui's Triangle." Later, Italian algebraist Niccolo Fontana Tartaglia put his

Pascal's Triangle up to row 7. Image courtesy of Wikipedia.

own spin on the Triangle, developing a formula for solving cubic polynomials—one hundred years before Pascal began his own work! Of course, Italians refer to it as "Tartaglia's Triangle" in homage to their countryman.

The interesting point is that, similar to pi, Pascal's Triangle is a formulaic sequence, a numeric description of repeating patterns that can look quite magical, especially when it was discovered by some of those ancient math wizards that the Fibonacci numbers were embedded within the Triangle. But similar to pi, there are sound mathematical properties underlying what some might look upon as a "number mystery."

Pascal's Triangle does indeed contain some eye-opening patterns:

- If one looks at the odd numbers only, you get what closely resembles the fractal known as Sierpinski Triangle, and the closer to infinity you get in the number of rows, the more it matches the Sierpinski Triangle.
- The value of each row, if each number in that row is considered as a decimal place and numbers over 9 are carried over, is a power of 11. Here again, the number 11 plays a significant role in mathematical patterns.

- By skipping over certain numbers at specific angles you get sums of Fibonacci numbers.
- Diagonals along the left and right edges contain only 1's.
- Diagonals next to the edge diagonals contain natural numbers in order.
- In rows where the second number is prime, all the terms in that row except the first 1's are multiples of that same prime number.

According to *goldennumber.net*, a few more interesting properties of Pascal's Triangle include:

- Horizontal rows add to powers of 2 (that is, 1, 2, 4, 8, 16, and so on).
- The horizontal rows represent powers of 11 (1, 11, 121, 1331, and so on).
- Adding any two successive numbers in the diagonal 1-3-6-10-15-21-28 . . . results in a perfect square (1, 4, 9, 16, and so on).
- It can be used to find combinations in probability problems (if, for instance, you pick any two of five items, the number of possible combinations is 10, found by looking in the second place of the fifth row. Do not count the 1s.)
- When the first number to the right of the 1 in any row is a prime number, all numbers in that row are divisible by that prime number.

Similar to the Fibonacci Sequence, Pascal's Triangle does hint at a "higher" intelligence behind its construction. Although numbers seem to have their own laws and rules, many mathematicians and scientists refuse to ascribe mystical powers to them. Perhaps they are shortsighted, for it seems that neither sacred numbers nor time prompts are enough to convince them of the magical powers of numbers. Or could it be that perhaps these rules and laws are more bland than we would like to think?

Here is a challenge we found on the website for Plus Magazine (*plus.maths.org*). Look up a bunch of naturally occurring numbers, such as the lengths of some of the world's rivers or the population sizes in Peruvian provinces. Take a sample of those naturally occurring numbers and look at their first digits (ignore zero for now). Then count how many numbers start with 1, how many start with 2, then 3, and so on.

Benford's Law

As you might expect, the end result would be that the same number of numbers begin with each differing digit, and that the proportion of numbers beginning with any of the specific digits between 1 and 9 would be 1/9. Right? Is that your final answer?

Wrong. The distribution of first digits is not so spread out, and, in fact, the most common starting digit will always be 1, while the least common is 9. Believe it or not, there is actually a formula that describes this, a law. Benford's Law, also known as "First-Digit Law." This law basically states that groups or lists of numbers from real-life sources will follow a specific pattern of leading digit frequency.

Canadian-American astronomer and mathematician Simon Newcomb (1835–1909) is credited as the first person to take notice of this amazing law. He wrote about it in his 1881 paper "Note on the Frequency of Use of the Different Digits in Natural Numbers." While Newcomb's observation was important, it was physicist Frank Benford that, in 1938 upon seeing the same patterns in his own research, finally put two and two together. Benford conducted some real-world experimental sampling, which was intended to prove the law that would later be named after him. He collected vast sums of data, including the addresses of the first 342 people listed in *American Men of Science*. In his analysis, he found that approximately 30 percent began with 1, 18 percent with 2, and so on. This pattern was repeatable with other sets of data, similar to baseball statistics, death rates, stock prices, street addresses, and electricity bills, but even Benford was at a loss to explain exactly why it worked.

Fast forward to around 1961, when American mathematician Roger Pinkham took the issue on. Pinkham believed that a potential explanation for this pattern could be explained. He supposed that there was indeed a law of "digit frequencies," and suggested that this law had to be universal—regardless of what form the digits were in; that is, prices in dollars or Drachma, or measurements in inches, cubits, or meters. Pinkham called this universality "scale invariant" and was the first to show that Benford's Law is, indeed, scale invariant. It works both ways, too. If a law of digit frequencies is scale invariant, it has to be Benford's Law.

Further experimentation with Benford's Law has been done on everything from business statistics and annual turnover rates to fundamental physical constants, but the law has some constraints. Numbers cannot be random, as in lottery picks (sorry!), and cannot be overly constrained where the range of possibilities is way too narrow. So while you cannot pick the winning numbers for next week's $50 million Power Lotto, you could use Benford's Law in other important ways.

Researchers are working on ways to use the law to detect fraud in tax returns and financial data as well as other useful functions, such as checking irregularities in clinical study trials and verifying demographic models.

Similar to all good things, the law does have specific limitations. Although it cannot apply to certain sets of numbers, it is an intriguing example of a mathematical formula that can be used to explain what might appear to some as "mysterious circumstances" involving the appearance of one digit over another in large sets of data.

> Benford's Law in Base 10 shows the percentage rate for each leading digit from 1 to 9.
>
> 1–30.1 percent
> 2–17.6 percent
> 3–12.5 percent
> 4–9.7 percent
> 5–7.9 percent
> 6–6.7 percent
> 7–5.8 percent
> 8–5.1 percent
> 9–4.6 percent

LAWS, RULES, AND CONSTANTS

There are literally dozens of such laws and rules that use numbers to define, categorize, and validate everything from computer processing to wide-scale distribution to human behavior. We don't have time to get into all of these in one chapter, but, to name a few:

- Apery's constant—A curious mathematical constant that arises in a variety of physical problems. The number of known digits of Apery's constant has increased dramatically during the last decades due to the utilization of computers and algorithmic enhancements.
- The Pareto Principle—named after economist Vilfredo Pareto, specifies that 80 percent of consequences come from 20 percent of the causes, or an unequal relationship between inputs and outputs. This principle serves as a general reminder that the relationship between inputs and outputs is not balanced. The Pareto Principle is also known as the Pareto Rule or the 80/20 Rule.
- Power Law—Any polynomial (a mathematical expression involving a sum of powers in one or more variables multiplied

by coefficients) relationship that exhibits the scale invariance property; power laws are involved in a huge number of natural patterns.

- Zipf's Law—Named for linguist George Zipf. It shows that the probability of occurrence of words or other items starts high and then decreases by tapering off. Thus, a few occur often while others occur rarely.

Again, these are just a few of the many laws, rules, and constants used in science, computing, business, physics, and even the determination of frequencies of particular earthquakes! Because this book deals so heavily with number patterns and synchronicity, we did find some specific laws that deal with things of a coincidental nature—things we often apply spiritual and personal meaning to.

Remember Littlewood's Law from chapter 7:7? The one that says each of us can expect a miracle to occur in our lives at a rate of about one per month? First published by Cambridge University professor J. E. Littlewood in *A Mathematician's Miscellany*, this law was initially developed to actually debunk supernatural or paranormal claims about the phenomenon of miracles. Littlewood's Law is directly related to the Law of Truly Large Numbers, which posits that when you get a sampling that is large enough, anything can happen. Consider it the Murphy's Law of Math.

Littlewood defines a miracle as "an exceptional event of special significance occurring at a frequency of one in a million; during the hours in which a human is awake and alert, a human will experience one thing per second (for instance, seeing the computer screen, the keyboard, the mouse, the article, and so on); additionally, a human is alert for about eight hours per day; and as a result, a human will, in thirty-five days, have experienced, under these suppositions, 1,008,000 things." Accepting this definition of a miracle, one can be expected to observe one miracle every thirty-five consecutive days or so. Therefore, miracles may not be as miraculous as originally thought! With so many people experiencing so many events throughout so many days, this seems not only logical, but far less "paranormal" than we've been led to believe by religious institutions that insist we have to beg, plead, and petition for just one miracle in a lifetime.

Again, we can't quite vouch for the effectiveness of this law in our own lives, but the Law of Truly Large Numbers does allow for strange coincidences, such as someone winning the lottery three times in a year. Yet there have actually been multiple studies conducted that help explain how this could easily happen. One of the most notable was conducted by statisticians Stephen Samuels and George McCabe of Purdue University after the *New York Times* ran a story of a woman who won the lottery twice, against staggering odds. According to their research, the odds of someone winning the lottery twice are actually about 1 in 30 in a four-month period, and better odds throughout a seven-year period. Not staggering at all. This is likely due to the fact that players tend to buy multiple tickets every week, upping their odds of winning considerably.

With more than six billion people on this planet, the odds are actually high that someone else, maybe even ten million someone elses, will be dreaming of the exact same thing you are tonight. Perhaps they will be having the same dinner. Or they share the same birth date. The larger the sample number, the more frequently these "coincidences" seem to occur, which appears astounding to us until we realize that just as many millions can share the same event, they can also share the same "meaningful coincidence," and apply the same personal significance to that event.

Thus, according to Littlewood's Law and the Law of Truly Large Numbers, each of us should be experiencing some strange, coincidental events, some even potentially miraculous, every single day. This would no doubt include seeing 11:11 on the clock or noticing the constant appearance of the number 23 throughout one's day, especially when our brains take the first few coincidences we experience and create patterns around them, amplifying their importance and setting us up to see even more and more of them. So, is this the explanation for the time prompt phenomena?

COINCIDENCE

Coincidence is described by author David Marks in his book *Psychology of the Psychic* as odd matches when two events occur that are perceived to contain a similarity. But as we have seen, Littlewood's Law and the Law of Truly Large Numbers dictate that these odd matches should actually be occurring all the time, just by the sheer size of our populace alone. Linked events happen every day, and the claims of paranormal or conspiratorial relationships may be overblown by the mere fact that life, and ultimately history, as mathematical laws suggest, repeats itself all the time. Statistically, coincidences must happen; they are inevitable.

Perhaps much of the reason humans apply so much meaning to these coincidences comes from our tendency toward matrixing, seeking patterns where there may or may not be any. If you recall, we talked briefly about the concept of matrixing in a previous chapter, as well as pareidolia, the human habit of looking for the familiar in the unfamiliar. We truly see and hear what we either want to see and hear ... or are biased towards seeing and hearing.

BIAS AND BELIEF

Ever have a spouse or loved one yell at you, "You only hear what you want to hear"? May we have a show of hands? This is a prime example of information bias in personal relationships—where we tend to tune out details or ignore red flags. Described as an "error of

> *History repeats itself. That's one of the things wrong with history.*
> —Clarence Darrow, U.S. defense lawyer (1857–1938)

inductive inference, or a form of selection bias toward confirmation of the hypothesis under study or disconfirmation of an alternative hypothesis," we have seen confirmation bias in action in our paranormal research, from folks on both sides of the fence. Believers shut out information that challenges their beliefs. Skeptics shut out information that challenges their disbelief.

Also referred to in psychology and cognitive science as "belief bias," "selective thinking," and "hypothesis locking," this variety of preconceived belief often lacks any supportive evidence, yet seems to again be related to our brain's ability to matrix and find relationships where none might really exist. We are sure that by now you won't be surprised to know that there is even a Murphy's Law of Research that states, "Enough research will tend to support your theory!"

This is similar to the "polarization effect" in politics and involves the use of evidence that can be described as neutral to shore up an established and biased existing point of view. The polarization of red versus blue-state beliefs is a perfect example of moving sides farther and farther apart as they cling for dear life onto confirmation biases that they perceive to support their beliefs. Again, we turn to the human brain and the five senses, which rapidly evaluate information and then "choose sides," so to speak, by filling in the gaps of unavailable, or shaky, information with a preexisting subconscious bias. Once the brain processes and accepts the bias as true, it becomes incredibly difficult to shake that bias, even upon presentation of true and valid information. Have you ever tried to convince a die-hard skeptic of something—even with undeniable proof? It is usually like talking to a wall.

These same dynamics occur when we consider whether or not we "believe" in psychics, ghosts, UFOs, and even whether we believe that numbers such as 11:11 have mystical meanings and connotations.

Geneticist David Perkins coined the phrase "myside bias" to refer to thinking "my" side of an argument is the correct one. This kind of thinking can lead to all sorts of negative psychological traits such as delusion, paranoia, and even self-aggrandization; however, here we are concerned with whether or not these biases are placing false assumptions on synchronistic events.

The tragic thing about these types of psychological biases is that even when someone is handed pure proof of evidence to the contrary, the human will to always "be right" usually kicks in, and we end up with often large groups of people following false leads and buying into inaccurate assumptions. Again, as paranormal researchers, we both see this happening every day, whether with people refusing to think orbs are nothing more than airborne particulate matter, or rigid scientists refusing to acknowledge that millions of people through time have seen ghosts, experienced time anomalies, or been visited by angelic beings in the dead of night.

The only way we can really discern the magical properties of numbers, and again, even Pythagoras and his ilk expounded upon them, is by suspending a little disbelief. We must engage in a little controlled confirmation bias and assume that behind the laws that seem to work with such precision—and shock with stunning accuracy—there had to have been a mind, a truly mathematical master genius, thinking all this stuff up.

Is God a number?

Chapter 10:10

IS GOD A NUMBER?

The great book of nature can be read only by those who know the language in which it was written. And this language is mathematics. —Galileo

Is God a number? At first glance, this might appear to be a loaded question that might elicit a similar response as to the question "Is God a male or female?" Of course, because Western religious traditions already insist that the answer to that controversial question is that God is male, let us attempt to transcend personal belief, and study the inquiry from a socio-religious perspective. Before doing so, however, it is important to recognize and comprehend the underlying idea and concept of God. Mohandas Karamchand Gandhi's poem "The Meaning of God" is a beautiful sonnet that describes God's ever-present nature:

> There is an indefinable mysterious Power that pervades everything.
> I feel It, though I do not see It.
> It is this unseen Power that makes Itself felt and yet defies all proof,
> because It is so unlike all that I perceive through my senses.
> It transcends the senses....
> That informing Power or Spirit is God....

> For I can see that in the midst of death life persists, in the
>   midst of untruth truth persists, in the midst of darkness
>   light persists.
> Hence I gather that God is Life, Truth, Light. He is love.
> He is supreme good.
> But he is no God who merely satisfies the intellect
> If He ever does.
> God to be God must rule the heart and transform it.
>
> —Mohandas Karamchand Gandhi
> (Young India, October 11, 1928)

Nearly every culture on Earth believes in the existence of some type of supreme higher power. From Yahweh to Yoda and the Force, the many changing faces of God remind us of the need to put our faith and belief in a bigger power that can watch over us, protect us, and guide us.

Although degrees of faith differ, the belief in "God" or a "Creator" is ubiquitous. Mankind's need for a foundational deity is universal, and it has often been credited with the creation and destruction of whole cultures. The "my God vs. your God" battle continues to this day, with no apparent end in sight.

Those who do believe in a God, though, strive to describe or define it, usually as an entity or figurehead and a deity that oversees the creation it manifested from its own desire to express itself. Omniscient, omnipotent, omnipresent—an all-encompassing force that, according to cultural belief, is either benevolent like a loving father or judgmental and harsh like a taskmaster.

Much has been written about various numbers that have been attributed to God throughout the ages. Among others, the numbers 1, 7, 40, 66, 180, and 360 have all been ascribed to be holy numbers with sacred meaning. The number 3, representing the triune nature of God, as well as the triune nature of reality itself, is found in a variety of religious traditions and creation myths, describing a three-fold nature to the creative force from which all else manifests; the seen and the unseen.

However, the idea that God itself could be described in numeric form seems almost blasphemous. To place divine power upon mere digits hints at heresy, as well as the blending of science with religion, which many feel go together about as well as oil and water. There do seem to be, though, certain numbers that hint at a significance far beyond ordinary mortal numbers. Aside from that, the creative force itself acts through various physical laws, and all laws have a mathematical component that cannot be denied at the fountain.

CONSTANTS

In chapter 8:8, we examined the cosmological constants of the six numbers that must be finely tuned to allow for life as we know it to exist. Add to this the cosmological constant of the presence of dark energy, a force that increases as the size of the universe increases, and we have measurable and demonstrable values that make up for all the matter, or lack of it, in the universe.

To fine-tune the physical constants present in the universe, including the four fundamental forces of gravitation, electromagnetism, and the strong and weak nuclear forces, as well as the ratio of electrons and protons present, requires something, or someone, to do the tuning. Could it all be a random accident that things worked out the way they did? Would that be easier to believe than the concept of a higher master mathematician at play, working out the equations that underlie the values that create stars, form galaxies, and allow for the birth of the elements from which life is made?

Many of the past and present leading scientists believe there is a God behind the number, if not a number behind the God. Here is a sampling of some quotes we found, with sources.

- Fred Hoyle (British astrophysicist): "A common sense interpretation of the facts suggests that a super intellect has monkeyed with physics, as well as with chemistry and biology, and that there are no blind forces worth speaking about in nature. The numbers one calculates from the facts seem to me so overwhelming as to put this conclusion almost beyond question." (*Wall Street Journal*, "Science Resurrects God," 12-27-97.)
- George Ellis (British astrophysicist): "Amazing fine tuning occurs in the laws that make this [complexity] possible. Realization of the complexity of what is accomplished makes it very difficult not to use the word miraculous without taking a stand as to the ontological status of the word." ("The Anthropic Principle," G. F. R. Ellis, 1993.)
- Paul Davies (British astrophysicist): "There is for me powerful evidence that there is something going on behind it all. . . . It seems as though somebody has fine-tuned nature's numbers to make the universe. . . . The impression of design is overwhelming." (*The Cosmic Blueprint: New Discoveries in Nature's Creative Ability to Order the Universe*, 1988.)
- Alan Sandage (winner of the Crawford Prize in astronomy): "I find it quite improbable that such order came out of chaos. There has to be some organizing principle. God to me is a mystery but is the explanation for the miracle of existence, why there is something instead of nothing." (*New York Times*, "Sizing Up the Cosmos," 03-12-91.)
- Arno Penzias (Nobel Prize in physics): "Astronomy leads us to a unique event, a universe which was created out of nothing, one with the very delicate balance needed to provide exactly the conditions required to permit life, and one which has an underlying (one might say 'supernatural') plan." (*Cosmos, Bios, Theos*, H. Margenau and R. A. Varghese, 1992.)

- Stephen Hawking (British astrophysicist): "Then we shall... be able to take part in the discussion of the question of why it is that we and the universe exist. If we find the answer to that, it would be the ultimate triumph of human reason—for then we would know the mind of God." (*A Brief History of Time*, 1988.)
- Alexander Polyakov (Soviet mathematician): "We know that nature is described by the best of all possible mathematics because God created it." ("Fortune," S. Gannes, 1986.)
- Ed Harrison (cosmologist): "Here is the cosmological proof of the existence of God—the design argument of Paley—updated and refurbished. The fine-tuning of the universe provides prima facie evidence of deistic design. Take your choice: blind chance that requires multitudes of universes or design that requires only one.... Many scientists, when they admit their views, incline toward the teleological or design argument." ("Masks of the Universe," E. Harrison, 1985.)
- Arthur L. Schawlow (professor of physics at Stanford University, 1981 Nobel Prize in physics): "It seems to me that when confronted with the marvels of life and the universe, one must ask why and not just how. The only possible answers are religious... I find a need for God in the universe and in my own life." (*Cosmos, Bios, Theos*, Margenau and Varghese, 1992.)
- Wernher von Braun (pioneer rocket engineer): "I find it as difficult to understand a scientist who does not acknowledge the presence of a superior rationality behind the existence of the universe as it is to comprehend a theologian who would deny the advances of science." (*The Skeptical Enquirer*, T. McIver, 1986.)

Though not all scientists would agree, this is but a sampling of those who are open to the presence of a higher force at play in the design of this finely tuned mechanism we call our universe. Most do agree that there is a numeric aspect, a degree of this fine-tuning required, and it can be described in numeric terms. And if these numbers are off by even the slightest amount, we cease to exist, or to ever have existed.

RUBIK'S CUBE

The numbers involved might be described better as the structure of the universe. These numeric values define laws, how things work, how they come about in the first place. We want to ask the questions: Is God a number, too? And if so, what number?

One of the most amusing and curious quests to find God's Number involves a classic toy: the Rubik's Cube. This little block of good fun requires the player to try to solve the puzzle by getting all the same colors on the same side of the cube. According to the World Cube Association website (yes, there are Olympics for cubing), the world record for "cubing" is currently 3.47 seconds, set in 2019.

According to Northeastern University researchers, who attempted to find the minimum number of moves possible to solve the cube (Ockham's razor meets Rubik's Cube), there are more than 43 quintillion possible arrangements to slush your way through. But a doctorate student named Dan Kunkle, and a professor of computer science named Gene Cooperman have announced that they found the "God Number," and it is 26. As part of a National Science Foundation grant, these two men solved Rubik's Cube in only 26 moves, what they call "God's Number," because it is assumed that any omniscient being would intuitively know the optimal steps required to solve any given configuration. (This assumes God has time to play with cube toys.)

The two plan to whittle down that God's Number, and they insist that the number is not what is important. Rather, the concept of finding the simplest and fastest way to solve a problem, with the use of technology, of course, as a powerful overseeing creator might.

OTHER POSSIBILITIES

Cool toys aside, there just might be a more serious number associated with the divine. The God numeral, according to physicist Scott Funkhouser, could be an unimaginably big number, say 10^{122}, or 10 times itself 122 times. This number seems to show up in some very critical cosmic instances, appearing first in the late 1990s when scientists began researching the presence of dark energy. This energy is believed to be behind the accelerating rate of expansion we see in our universe. This same number, albeit with a give-or-take of a factor of 10, appears in other important ratios, such as the ratio of mass of the observable universe to that of the smallest "quantum" of mass, which is 6×10^{121}; and one of the measurements of entropy that determines the many ways particles in the current universe can be spatially arranged, which is 2.5×10^{122}.

Again, even to see these common ratios show up five or six times is stunning to most physicists and cosmologists. It seems highly unlikely that chance is behind this repetition of ratios involving huge numbers, or that it's akin to rolling the dice and playing a huge game of cosmic craps. Sir James Joyce, considered by many to be one of the founders of astrophysics, once wrote that the universe seemed to him more like a great thought than a great machine. This begs the question: Who or what is thinking the great thought?

TELEOLOGICAL ARGUMENT

This desire to find evidence of an existence of a creator or Godlike power in the perceived order and design of nature is called a "teleological argument," or an "argument from design," and is based upon the Greek word *telos*, meaning "end" or "purpose." The argument consists of four basic components:

- Nature appears too orderly, complex, and purposeful to be random or accidental.
- Nature must have been created by an intelligent, wise, and purposeful entity.
- God is intelligent, wise, and purposeful.
- God exists, and nature is proof.

The problems arise, though, when the argument extends into a definition of intelligence, and religious connotations become involved. In our discussion of Information Theory, we looked at a theory that offers a compromise. The universe looks ordered and purposeful because it is a giant computer computing itself. Most people might not equate a computer with God, but this theory allows for intelligent design behind the numbers and values that make up our universe, as well as a non-religious sensibility. The teleological argument buys into the Anthropic Principle, which proposes that the finely tuned constants are set to specifically allow for life as we know it; namely, intelligent life that evolves into human beings.

The main forces behind the Anthropic Principle are John D. Barrow and Frank J. Tipler, authors of *The Anthropic Cosmological Principle*. They propose that the intricacy of design that leads to life is utterly improbable and must be on purpose, compared to the vast and infinite range of possible conditions that could have led to the opposite result: no life at all. But other scientists argue that statistics could be manipulated to define a number of natural situations that have that same level of improbability yet happened anyway. Life may, then, not be as improbable as we think. Thus, maybe the conditions that arose on earth as sustainable to life were quite simply luck... just as picking a one in a million lottery ticket might be.

Proponents of the teleological argument must therefore prove that only intelligent design, and not sheer luck, could account for a universe so perfectly tuned and masterfully thought out, and opponents suggest that even if there is an intelligent force behind this whole mathematically inclined reality, it does not mean that designer is God. In the words of author Richard Dawkins (*The God Delusion*, *The Blind Watchmaker*), it is only required that the designer be at least as complex and purposeful as the designed object. This does not imply the designer is God, and French philosopher Voltaire himself echoed this sentiment in his belief that the teleological argument suggested a powerful intelligence, but not necessarily the *most* powerful one.

There is even argument over the nature of the designer itself. According to Quentin Smith, author of the article "The Anthropic Coincidences, Evil and the Disconfirmation of Theism", we should not even assume that the designer of any intelligent universe would be a good guy. Instead, he warns us "it is reasonable to conclude that God does not exist, since God is omnipotent, omniscient, and perfectly good and thereby would not permit any gratuitous natural evil. But since gratuitous natural evils are precisely what we would expect if a malevolent spirit created the universe... if any spirit created the universe, it is malevolent." The universe, Smith argues, is a hostile environment indeed, with most of its conditions not at all gently attuned to the emergence of life.

This hostility is evident even when examining the way nature works on our own planet, with the survival of the fittest and the food chain. It's not necessarily a dog-eat-dog world, but it definitely is one where shark eats fish, leopard eats gazelle, and humans eat whatever they fancy. On a more macrocosmic level, the hostility of the environments on other planets do not even lend themselves to life, and one can only imagine how difficult it would be for anything to survive the extremes of heat and cold to be found in the outer reaches of our universe.

A HIGHER NATURE

As the battle rages on over whether or not the universe was designed with purpose, intent, and even intelligence, pitting science against religion in a most current sense, there are compromises being offered between those who walk in either world. Some scientists and religious leaders see no conflict between the concepts of evolution and intelligent design, rather choosing to view the existence of life on Earth as something potentially arising from a creator-deity who utilizes evolution as the means of allowing life to unfold and emerge and evolve.

With continued conflict and controversy surrounding the basic existence of God, it would seem even more impossible to quantify the nature of God, especially in mathematical terms. But numerologists and those involved with Sacred Geometry think that there are sequences, such as the God Number of 112358134711, which speak of a higher and more profound nature. This number, linked to the Kabbalah and the Fibonacci Sequence discussed earlier, always comes back to the master number of 11. You start with the number 1, and then add each number to the one before it to get the next number. 0 + 1 = 1. 1 + 1 = 2. 2 + 1 = 3. 3 + 2 = 5. 5 + 3 = 8, and so on to 7 + 4 = 11, and then the whole thing repeats itself. Numerologists claim if you add up the series of numbers 1123581347 (which we visited in an earlier chapter), without the final 11, you get 8, the number of eternity and infinity, and if you allow the 11 to repeat all the way to the end, you end on 10, the divine number and a magical number rife with symbolism in the Kabbalah, Gematria, and even the Tarot. While this speaks volumes to numerologists, to others it seems as though any end number could be given some mysterious, even divine, significance.

333

Christians point to the number 333 as being the number of God. We recall 666 is the number of God's adversary, the Beast of Revelation, the anti-Christ of the Apocalypse. The number 333 is considered holy because of the divine nature of the triune, tripled. The number 3, as presented in earlier chapters, holds such a high place in the numerological hierarchy of numbers, and tripling imbues it with a profound holiness and power. God becomes "three times holy" as in Isaiah 6:3.

777

Perhaps the God Number exists far closer to home than the outer reaches of an expanding universe. In the first chapter of this book, we looked at time prompts and how they might be wake-up calls meant to, as one theory states, activate our "junk DNA." If the universe is a giant computer spitting out its and bits of information to create reality, then our DNA is a personal computer doing the same thing, only the its and bits it spits out make . . . us.

Others involved in Bible Code interpretation and sacred numbers in the Old and New Testament suggest that perhaps God's Number should be 777, the triplicate of the divine and lucky number 7.

GEOMETRIC HARMONY

Author Sarah Voss writes in her book *What Number Is God? Metaphors, Metaphysics, Metamathematics, and the Nature of Things* that the concept of a divine number might be more metaphorical than literal. She agrees that all of life is deeply imbued with the presence of sacred numbers, geometry, and patterns, and that we might need to take a more metaphorical approach to seeking a distinct divine numeric association with the higher intelligence thought to be behind all of creation. She quotes Dutch mathematician B. L. van der Waerden, in reference to the Pythagorean Greeks who revered numbers as divine, as saying, "Mathematics formed a part of their religion. Their doctrine proclaims that God has ordered the universe by means of numbers. God is unity, the world a plurality, and it consists of contrasting elements. It is harmony which restores unity to the contrasting parts and which molds them into a cosmos. Harmony is divine. It consists of numerical ratios."

The geometric harmony spoken of, Voss continues, is present throughout the physical world, in symmetries and proportions evident throughout nature. These proportions are mirrors of the grander, greater macrocosmic reality, symbols of the cosmos seen in the intricacies of a spiraled face of a flower or a nautilus shell. But she suggests that Pythagoras, Plato, and others may have been speaking metaphorically when they described nature and natural laws in terms of geometrical ratios and proportions. Yet many of the scientists of the past have acknowledged that this link between macro and micro, between numbers and nature, does also exist in a literal sense, even though it may have been written about and philosophized about in more symbolic terms.

DNA

One of the most enduring symbols that suggest a higher intelligence instilled in the structure of manifest reality is within our own bodies. DNA operates a lot like a computer, and the human genome consists of the equivalent of 750 megabytes of information or data. A very small percentage of that data, perhaps 3 percent, is involved in the composition of the 22,000-plus genes that make each of us the person that we are. The other 97 percent is like a blank hard drive, ready to be encoded with information to store in the genome.

This non-coding DNA is often referred to as "junk DNA," although in recent years it has been determined to be anything but, both by the scientific community and the metaphysical community. A question on one intelligent-design website (*www.godandscience .org*) begs for more argument: "Why would a perfect God create flawed DNA which is primarily composed of useless, non-coding regions?" Yet, as mentioned earlier, God does indeed create flaws throughout nature—if we interpret them as such. Maybe what we see as flaws are really all a part of a bigger picture to which we are only given a tiny glimpse.

We look at the 3 percent of DNA that works with amazing and intricate precision to create the elements of our bodies, from cells to major organs, and then directs those elements in just the precise manner. To someone with a religious bent, the fact that our bodies are mechanisms of the highest and most profound design and order are Godlike enough. DNA makes each of us who we are; unique expressions of life itself, yet in the most fundamental way, all pretty much the same.

But it's the junk stuff that interests those who experience time prompts, and it's the junk stuff that suggests there might be more to us humans than we ever imagined, more to us than our blue eyes and brown hair and long legs and crooked smiles. Most geneticists agree that the non-coding DNA is necessary for the proper functioning of the coded DNA. They are just not sure how. There are many theories as to why the non-coding DNA appears inactive, even suggesting it provided no selective advantages or that it was once a necessity and lost its coding ability somewhere along the way. Truth is, it is still within us, and the quest is on to determine what it just might be capable of doing if activated.

Also known as "secondary DNA," many studies have shown that what we thought was junk plays a functional role in the structure of the nucleus of a cell, and that the amount of this non-coding DNA was directly proportional to the size of the cell. Other studies showed that heterochromatin, once believed to be junk DNA, actually has a role in suppressing genes, and that actual gene expression during development is also related to non-coding DNA. This DNA seems to have more functionality than ever imagined, providing regulation of certain roles in the development and proper framing of the translation of proteins. Further research is revealing even more amazing functions of what was once thought to be dormant or inactive stuff, and its role in making sure our metabolic system works as it should.

Humans aren't the only holders of junk DNA. A study by David Haussler of UC California, Santa Cruz, reported by the BBC, showed that humans, rats, and mice share "many identical chunks of apparently 'junk' DNA." The team Haussler led compared the genome sequence of humans with that of mice and rats, and they were literally astonished by the identical stretches of DNA they found across the three species. Furthermore, they found that the patterns matched closely with chickens, dogs, and fish sequences.

These "ultra-conserved elements" that did not seem to do anything of value suggested that their function was indeed of great importance, most likely, as Haussler stated, by controlling "the activity of indispensable genes and embryo development." The study led many scientists to rethink their opinion of this junk stuff, prompting Professor Chris Ponting of the UK Medical Research Council's Functional Genetics Unit to state, "I think other bits of 'junk' DNA will turn out not to be junk. I think this is the tip of the iceberg, and that there will be many more similar findings."

For many people who experience time prompts, the theory is that the awakening of a deeper consciousness and awareness is one of those findings lying just beneath the tip of the iceberg. There is even a hint of a "language" to this non-coding DNA, as pointed out in a *Science* magazine article by F. Flam, which suggested that the sequence of the "syllables," or the nucleotides in DNA, should be completely random but are not. They in fact have a striking parallel with human language and are now believed to contain some kind of coded information. The authors of this paper, called "Hints of a Language in Junk DNA," actually employed a series of linguistics tests to analyze the junk DNA and found amazing similarities to human language. Again, the cry arose that there would be no beneficial reason for an organism to carry around so many useless, junk molecules that seemingly served no purpose. There must be a code. There must be a purpose to that code. The quest is on to determine what that code is trying to tell us, and how it will change us or transform us, once awakened into its full capacity.

This code, and its purpose, is not yet fully understood in the science community. But the spiritual community is hard on the case, suggesting that this non-coding DNA is the home of psychic abilities, paranormal manifestation, and higher levels of conscious awareness waiting to be awakened in humankind. From seeing ghosts to being able to know what another person is thinking, to locating a missing child using psi abilities, this code might hold the key to the realm of the unknown that we have long relegated to the fringes of science, or, better yet, the world of pseudoscience.

Though there is no physical evidence for this, many people feel strongly that this part of the makeup of the human body is where the "key" to higher levels of being lies, and that the door is a trigger event that will activate this DNA and allow it to fulfill its purpose, thus allowing us as a species to fulfill ours. This may also turn out to be the case for the other living species that share with us the secret of junk, or unfulfilled, DNA. We may not be the only ones ascending!

THE HERMETIC CODE

In his book *The Hermetic Code in DNA: The Sacred Principles in the Ordering of the Universe*, Michael Hayes suggests there is a mathematical-based code embedded throughout ancient religions and traditions and science, a code that is mirrored in our own DNA structure. He calls it the Hermetic Code, and states, "The Hermetic Code is much more than a mathematical tool. It is a universal blueprint for all evolutionary or creative development, and its distinctive inner symmetry is to be found in the biomolecular and physical structures of all form of life."

The Hermetic Code is based upon the "sixty-four word/twenty-two note amino acid 'scale of resonance' but also, for example, in the overall physiology of human beings with their three nerve complexes responsible for sensation, emotion, and perception, and their eight sets of endocrine transformers. . . ." Hayes, also the author of *The Infinite Harmony*, posits that all living beings are "hermetically composed; they are all in their relative scales evolutionary 'triple octaves' with the inherent potential to achieve a state of 'optimum resonance.'" It is this optimum resonant state that many believe will be the result of our junk DNA being triggered into activity.

Hayes also asks the important question of "who or what told DNA how to behave?" His theory of an association between our DNA and a higher mathematical code that shows symmetries between what goes on "above" in the cosmos and what goes on "below" in our own physiology is behind the idea that it is possible, through "transcendental evolution," for human individuals to emulate the living cell and to achieve a similar condition of optimum resonance.

Though quick to admit that the evolution of DNA on earth has been a bit dicey, and often erratic, Hayes states, ". . . underlying all this apparent random, selective evolution is the symmetry of DNA and the genetic code" and compares that symmetry to fundamental laws found in nature, especially those found in harmonics that make up the "music" of life. The harmonic ratios of music mirror the ordering principles of the universe . . . and our own DNA. As above, so below . . . as if a "fundamental cosmic harmony" was behind it all. And, of course, this harmony is based upon numbers. He even quotes physicist Paul Davies, who said, "We can therefore regard the spectrum of light from an atom as similar to the sound of a musical instrument," and takes it one step further by describing a range of musical relationships between atoms and their components, even referring to the theory of quantum chromodynamics, which suggests that beneath the material of an atom "there are other essentially musical symphonies being played by nature."

Anyone who has studied music theory knows of the prominence of mathematics in scales, octaves, and such. According to Hayes, "The Hermetic Code, as we know, is primarily an expression of the law of triple creation, which holds that everything is composed of trinities within trinities. This means that the three individual octaves embodied with pi are in themselves triple octaves, making nine octaves in total, or sixty-four 'notes'—precisely the number of RNA codon combinations."

Okay, so God may be both a mathematician *and* a musician, not to mention a geneticist and computer programming whiz! DNA molecules work with four chemical components, known as bases of the genetic code, which construct molecules known as RNA triplet codons. Each of those comprises three bases, serving as templates, Hayes explains, for the production of amino acids, which in turn assemble into complex protein chains. All of this follows the musical structure evident in the formula pi, and seen throughout nature and the cosmos on an even grander scale. But Hayes also suggests that this Hermetic Code is genetic, and that "certain fundamental aspects of consciousness—ideas, concepts, revelations, and so forth—are metaphysical genes and are produced in exactly the same way as are amino-acid chains."

This more metaphysical attribute to both non-coded DNA and the idea of a higher intelligence behind man and nature alike is what those who experience 11:11 time prompts believe will lead to a coming age of higher reality. If DNA serves to evolve us physically, could the secrets it holds within its own "King's Chamber" serve to evolve us spiritually and consciously as well? The concept of resonance, of the links between vibration and levels of consciousness, cannot be ignored either. Are we all on the cusp of a spiritual revolution that will be brought about by the activation of our 97 percent non-coding DNA, where a Hermetic Code based upon the fundamentals of music and harmony sits?

If the universe is indeed "one song," maybe this is the song we are all about to sing, once we all find our individual and collective voice.

BOND OF NUMBER

Throughout this book, it has been made clear that the underlying dynamics of nature and even humanity is based upon mathematical laws. These laws may make up part of the Theory of Everything sought after by physicists, yet go one step further, as stated by John Michell in *The Dimensions of Paradise*. Ancient scientific metaphysics had a similar but wider function. It attempted to describe not merely the nature of the physical universe but human nature also, and in the same terms, linking the two together as macrocosmic and microcosmic aspects of the one primordial act of creation. The universe, human nature, and the mind of the Creator were made commensurable by number, which Plato called the "bond holding all things together."

This bond of number was seen in ancient traditions as being applicable to both individual human existence and the greater design of the cosmos, and it was just as functional and present in the DNA that makes us who we are as it was in the fine-tuned structure of the planets and galaxies and stars. This rather sacred concept, as Michell concludes, is a "synthesis of the proportions and harmonies in the field of number, it depicts the essential structure of the universe and the human mind alike...." It describes the dimensions of both a pyramid and the heavens themselves and dictates the form of human and animal and plant, all according to a great and grand design that includes both randomness, at times, and perfect order at others, as part of a whole working to create life. Successfully, we might add!

Numbers influence us and govern our lives. They have their own power, and that power just might be divine in nature. They shape the laws that shape us and, amplified by the meaning we give them, make our reality real. God may not be a particular digit, sequence, or even code. Instead, the creative and intelligent foundation from which all reality springs forth appears to be enamored of numbers, using them to shape the laws that shape form, matter, and energy, and dictate the way things appear to be, seen and unseen, in this and any other universe.

God is not a number. God is all numbers . . . and numbers are everything.

Chapter 11:11

WHY NUMBERS MATTER

I could never make out what those damn dots meant...
—*Lord Randolph Churchill,*
on figuring out decimal points

When we began this book, neither of us truly had any idea just how important numbers were. Of course we knew they played a role in our everyday lives, especially when we pulled out our ATM card or checkbook, dialed a critical phone number, or filled in our Social Security number on an application. We were certainly aware of the proliferation of numbers all around us. What we weren't fully cognizant of was the magnitude. Numbers literally are anywhere and everywhere.

Throughout our research and discussion with others, we came away with a new appreciation for numbers, as well as a stunning discovery: numbers are magical, and they matter. Sometimes more than we ever imagined. Numbers have the power to shape, form, describe, manifest, and transform. Numbers truly are the key to the universe.

Numbers have the power to transcend suffering and usher in a new era of possibilities. But, similar to miracle diets or mail-order brides, there is a catch.

In her book *Numbers*, written with David Boyle, Dame Anita Roddick reminds us that "we are measured, counted, and recorded every time we buy anything. We are summed up, averaged out and cross-sectioned by academics and officials in surveys and screeds of government statistics that suck us dry of our individuality. We are part of a gigantic experiment that believes everything can be measured . . ." But Roddick did go on to emphasize that numbers are magic—if, and only if, we remember that what they quantify and represent is us. The measure of a man or a woman. Humanity.

And therein lies the catch: The best things in life are not only free but immeasurable. Love. Passion. Hope. Beauty. Goodness. Humor. Character.

Perhaps it is best to think of numbers the same way that we do the houses in which we live. They provide a foundation and shelter within which we move and live. They give us structure, familiarity, and a sense of home. Outside their walls, we find those things to which only numbers can allude. The mysteries of life that, when reduced to mathematical equations, suddenly lose their mystery and mystique.

Thus, the question: With so much technological gadgetry at our disposal, and our dependence on money, stock performances, dates, and times . . . with all of our obsession with ages and years and breast size and waist width and how many hairs remain on our heads, are we placing too much importance on the numbers and not enough on the actual things they measure? Are we forgetting about life itself?

For all of us who have had unusual experiences with numbers, especially those mysterious and sometimes annoying time prompts, we need to remember that it is not the digits themselves that matter, but what the digits are alerting us to. Pay attention. Wake up. Take notice.

Seeing 11:11 on the clock day after day, night after night, is not coincidental. It is not just a random event that miraculously keeps repeating. It happens for a reason. Unfortunately, we still don't know what that reason is.

As one woman so succinctly wrote on *Angelscribe.com*, "I have been having some weird experiences with the 1111, 111, and others. I have been noticing them for about a week now. It is so weird. I will look at the clock and it's 1:11. Today I was trying to change some properties on my web browser and the file size was 1111 bytes! That was really weird. I went back and looked again and it was different! Weird! I have seen a lot of the double numbers and numbers with the 111's. Obviously, someone is trying to tell me something. I figure I will learn that something soon."

Yes, we all may learn "that something" soon. Maybe, when we learn "that something," it will transform us and enlighten us, both individually and collectively.

Whatever these time prompts mean, and whatever these strange signs, sequences, or synchronicities are trying to tell us, the bottom line is, no matter what the circumstances, we must pay attention to our lives. We must live in the now.

Something or someone is trying to get us to look away from the cell phones, computers, video games, and awful reality shows where we watch people play out their own lives for the camera, while ignoring the sheer potentiality of our own. It is truly incredible to think that the "someone" or "something" may be an internal influence originating within our own brains, or perhaps it is a subconscious poke in the side from some higher (or lower!) dimensional being. Remember this the next time your cell phone rings or alerts you to a text message.

The "who" or "what" matters not—the fact that we are being prompted in the first place is the truly important facet of the equation.

Time prompts may be occurring in the life of every human being every day, but not every human being pays the needed attention. With all of the background noise and static in our lives, it's quite probable that the vast majority just aren't aware because they have mentally "tuned" them out, just as many of us tune out other synchronicities. The tragic thing is, by ignoring these "higher" bits of potential information, we might be shooting ourselves in the foot on a much grander scale. Do we live just for getting by in the present, or with one eye on the future? Do we merely survive, or attempt to thrive?

The fact that these time prompts happen to each of us in a personalized and individualized manner that holds a specific meaning is critical. Whatever is behind this, brain or divine, it knows just what each of us needs to actually wake up and take notice and will continue to prod and poke at us until we do. Imagine millions of souls moving forward, each of them on a separate path all their own, yet linked by an invisible cord.

The numbers behind the time prompts are the cord.

Appendix

NUMBER TRIVIA AND ANOMALIES

Before we ended this book, we simply could not resist a little fun with numbers. Because as mysterious and enigmatic as they are, they can also bring out a gasp of awe or a chuckle or two. Following are some of the amazing anomalies we found on the Internet and in other sources that show, indeed, that there is more to numbers than originally meets the eye. Some of the following information is anecdotal and should not be taken as absolute fact.

0 TO 50—UNIQUE NUMBER FACTS

- 0 is the additive identity.
- 1 is the multiplicative identity.
- 2 is the only even prime.
- 3 is the number of spatial dimensions we live in.
- 4 is the smallest number of colors sufficient to color all planar maps.
- 5 is the number of Platonic solids.
- 6 is the smallest perfect number.
- 7 is the smallest number of faces of a regular polygon that is not constructible by straightedge and compass.

- 8 is the largest cube in the Fibonacci sequence.
- 9 is the maximum number of cubes that are needed to sum to any positive integer.
- 10 is the base of our number system.
- 11 is the largest known multiplicative persistence.
- 12 is the smallest abundant number.
- 13 is the number of Archimedian solids.
- 14 is the smallest number n with the property that there are no numbers relatively prime to n smaller numbers.
- 15 is the smallest composite number n with the property that there is only one group of order n.
- 16 is the only number of the form xy = yx with x and y different integers.
- 17 is the number of wallpaper groups.
- 18 is the only number (other than 0) that is twice the sum of its digits.
- 19 is the maximum number of fourth powers needed to sum to any number.
- 20 is the number of rooted trees with six vertices.
- 21 is the smallest number of distinct squares needed to tile a square.
- 22 is the number of partitions of eight.
- 23 is the smallest number of integer-sided boxes that tile a box so that no two boxes share a common length.
- 24 is the largest number divisible by all numbers less than its square root.
- 25 is the smallest square that can be written as a sum of two squares.
- 26 is the only positive number to be directly between a square and a cube.
- 27 is the largest number that is the sum of the digits of its cube.
- 28 is the second perfect number.

- 29 is the seventh Lucas number.
- 30 is the largest number with the property that all smaller numbers relatively prime to it are prime.
- 31 is a Mersenne prime.
- 32 is the smallest non-trivial fifth power.
- 33 is the largest number that is not a sum of distinct triangular numbers.
- 34 is the smallest number with the property that it and its neighbors have the same number of divisors.
- 35 is the number of hexominoes.
- 36 is the smallest non-trivial number that is both square and triangular.
- 37 is the maximum number of fifth powers needed to sum to any number.
- 38 is the last Roman numeral when written lexicographically.
- 39 is the smallest number that has three different partitions into three parts with the same product.
- 40 is the only number whose letters are in alphabetical order.
- 41 is a value of n so that $x^2 + x + n$ takes on prime values for x = 0, 1, 2, ... n-2.
- 42 is the fifth Catalan number.
- 43 is the number of sided seven-iamonds.
- 44 is the number of derangements of five items.
- 45 is a Kaprekar number.
- 46 is the number of different arrangements (up to rotation and reflection) of nine non-attacking queens on a 9 × 9 chessboard.
- 47 is the largest number of cubes that cannot tile a cube.
- 48 is the smallest number with 10 divisors.
- 49 is the smallest number with the property that it and its neighbors are squareful.
- 50 is the smallest number that can be written as the sum of two squares in two ways.

MORE FUN FACTOIDS

- 123456787654321 is 11,111,111 multiplied by itself.
- On a bingo card of 90 numbers there are approximately 44 million possible ways to make bingo.
- The number 2,520 can be divided by 1, 2, 3, 4, 5, 6, 7, 8, 9, and 10 without having a fractional leftover.
- The chances of an exact duplication of fingerprints are about 64 billion to 1.
- The odds against a royal flush in poker are exactly 649,739 to 1.
- A sneeze can travel as fast as 100 miles per hour.
- If you had $10 billion in $1 bills and spent one every second, it would take 317 years to spend them all.
- Six eight-stud Lego pieces can be combined 102,981,500 ways.
- If you had 15 cubes numbered 1 to 15 and you tried to line them up in every possible sequence, and if you made a change every minute, it would take you 2,487,996 years to do it.
- Except for 2 and 3, every prime number will eventually become divisible by 6 if you either add or subtract 1 from the number. For example, the number 17, plus 1, is divisible by 6. The number 19, minus 1, is also divisible by 6.
- If you were to go on vacation for 11 days, you'd have less than one million seconds to enjoy it.
- The number of possible ways of playing just the first four moves on each side in a game of chess is 318,979,564,000.
- There are 24 known "perfect" numbers. These are numbers that equal the sum of all its divisors except itself. For instance, 6—the lowest of these numbers—is divisible by 1, 2, or 3 and 1 + 2 + 3 = 6. The largest of the known "perfect" numbers has 12,003 digits.
- The numbers on opposite sides of a die always add up to 7.

SPOOKY COINCIDENCES: THE LINCOLN-KENNEDY LINKS

- Abraham Lincoln was elected to Congress in 1846.
- John F. Kennedy was elected to Congress in 1946.
- Abraham Lincoln was elected president in 1860.
- John F. Kennedy was elected president in 1960.
- Both were particularly concerned with civil rights.
- Both presidents were shot on a Friday.
- Both presidents were shot in the head.
- Lincoln's secretary was named Kennedy.
- Kennedy's secretary was named Lincoln.
- Both were assassinated by Southerners.
- Both were succeeded by Southerners named Johnson.
- Andrew Johnson, who succeeded Lincoln, was born in 1808.
- Lyndon Johnson, who succeeded Kennedy, was born in 1908.
- John Wilkes Booth, who assassinated Lincoln, was born in 1839.
- Lee Harvey Oswald, who assassinated Kennedy, was born in 1939.
- Both assassins were known by their three names.
- Both names are composed of 15 letters.
- Lincoln was shot at the theater named "Ford."
- Kennedy was shot in a car called "Lincoln" made by Ford.
- Lincoln was shot in a theater, and his assassin ran and hid in a warehouse.
- Kennedy was shot from a warehouse, and his assassin ran and hid in a theater.
- Booth and Oswald were assassinated before their trials.
- A week before Lincoln was shot, he was in Monroe, Maryland.
- A week before Kennedy was shot, he was with Marilyn Monroe.

- Lincoln's name has seven letters.
- Kennedy's name has seven letters.
- In Lincoln's and Kennedy's names the vowels and consonants fall in exactly the same place; in the order c, v, c, c, v, c, c.
- War was thrust upon Lincoln almost immediately after inauguration.
- War was thrust upon Kennedy almost immediately after inauguration.
- Lincoln ordered the Treasury to print its own money.
- Kennedy ordered the Treasury to print its own money.
- International bankers may have arranged the assassinations of Lincoln and Kennedy.
- Lincoln gave negroes freedom and legalized equality.
- Kennedy enforced equality for negroes.
- Lincoln delivered the Gettysburg Address on November 19, 1863.
- Kennedy was assassinated on November 22, 1963.
- Lincoln was sitting beside his wife when he was shot.
- Kennedy was sitting beside his wife when he was shot.
- Rathbone, who was with Lincoln when he was shot, was injured (by being stabbed).
- Connally, who was with Kennedy when he was shot, was injured (by being shot).
- Rathbone's name has eight letters.
- Connally's name has eight letters.
- Lincoln's bodyguard was away from his post at the door of the president's box at the theatre.
- Kennedy's bodyguards were away from their posts on the running-boards of the president's car.
- Lincoln didn't die immediately after being shot.
- Kennedy didn't die immediately after being shot.

- Lincoln and Kennedy died in places beginning with the initials P and H.
- Lincoln died in Petersen's house.
- Kennedy died in Parkland Hospital.
- There were conspiracy theories that Johnson had knowledgeable about Lincoln's assassination.
- There were conspiracy theories that Johnson had knowledgeable about Kennedy's assassination.
- Days before it happened, Lincoln told his wife and friends about a dream he'd had of being shot by an assassin.
- Hours before it happened, Kennedy told his wife and friends it would be easy for an assassin to shoot him from a crowd.
- Shortly after Lincoln was shot, the telegraph system went down.
- Shortly after Kennedy was shot, the telephone system went down.
- Kennedy's father had been the Ambassador to England at the Court of St. James's.
- Lincoln's son became the Ambassador to England at the Court of St. James's.
- Lincoln's wife tastefully and expensively redecorated the White House.
- Kennedy's wife tastefully and expensively redecorated the White House.
- Lincoln loved great literature and could recite poetry by heart.
- Kennedy loved great literature and could recite poetry by heart.
- Lincoln had young children while living at the White House.
- Kennedy had young children while living at the White House.
- Lincoln's sons had ponies they rode on the White House grounds.

- Kennedy's daughter had a pony she rode on the White House grounds.
- Lincoln lost a child (12-year-old son) while president.
- Kennedy lost a child (newly born son) while president.
- Lincoln had two sons named Robert and Edward. Edward died young and Robert lived on.
- Kennedy had two brothers named Robert and Edward. Robert died young and Edward lived on.
- Lincoln's funeral train traveled from Washington, DC, to New York.
- Kennedy's brother's funeral train traveled from New York to Washington, DC.
- The man running alongside Kennedy's car snapping pictures with his 35mm camera was a salesman of Lincoln cars.
- Kennedy bought a Virginia home that was the 1861 Civil War headquarters of Lincoln's first general-in-chief, McClellan.
- Jefferson Davis was the name of the president of the Confederate states while Lincoln was president of the Union states.
- Jefferson Davis Tippit was the name of the police officer killed allegedly by Kennedy's alleged assassin.
- Lincoln was sitting in a rocking chair at Ford's Theater when he was shot.
- Kennedy had a special rocking chair he sat in at the White House.
- Henry Ford bought the rocking chair Lincoln died in and put it in his museum in Dearborn.
- Kennedy's seat in the Lincoln he was sitting in when he was shot is in Ford's museum.
- Lincoln's seat in the Ford's Theater he was sitting in when he was shot is in Ford's museum.

DYSCALCULIA—A NUMBER DISEASE?

Dyscalculia is a type of specific learning disability (SLD) involving innate difficulty in learning or comprehending mathematics. Dyscalculia is a lesser-known disability, similar and potentially related to dyslexia and Developmental Dyspraxia. Dyscalculia occurs in people across the whole IQ range, and sufferers often, but not always, also have difficulties with time, measurement, and spatial reasoning. Current estimates suggest it may affect about 5 percent of the population. Although some researchers believe that dyscalculia necessarily implies mathematical reasoning difficulties as well as difficulties with arithmetic operations, there is evidence (especially from brain-damaged patients) that arithmetic (for example, calculation and number fact memory) and mathematical (abstract reasoning with numbers) abilities can be dissociated. That is (some researchers argue), an individual might suffer arithmetic difficulties (or dyscalculia) with no impairment of, or even giftedness in, abstract mathematical reasoning abilities.

The word *dyscalculia* comes from Greek and Latin, which means: "counting badly." The prefix *dys* comes from Greek and means "badly." *Calculia* comes from the Latin "calculare" which means "to count." That word *calculare* again comes from "calculus," which means "pebble" or one of the counters on an abacus. Frequent difficulties with arithmetic, confusing the signs: +, -, ÷, and ×.

Other signs:

- Inability to tell which of two numbers is the larger.
- Difficulty with everyday tasks such as checking change and reading analog clocks.

- Inability to comprehend financial planning or budgeting, sometimes even at a basic level; for example, estimating the cost of the items in a shopping basket or balancing a checkbook.
- Difficulty with times-tables, mental arithmetic, etc.
- Require logic rather than formulae, until a higher level requiring calculations is obtained.
- Difficulty with conceptualizing time and judging the passing of time.
- Problems differentiating between left and right.
- Having a poor sense of direction (that is, north, south, east, and west), potentially even with a compass.
- Difficulty navigating or mentally "turning" the map to face the current direction rather than the common North = Top usage.
- Having difficulty mentally estimating the measurement of an object or distance (for example, whether something is 10 or 20 feet [3 or 6 meters] away).
- Inability to grasp and remember mathematical concepts, rules, formulae, and sequences.
- An inability to read a sequence of numbers, or transposing them when repeated, such as turning 56 into 65.
- Difficulty keeping score during games.
- Difficulty with games, such as poker, with more flexible rules for scoring.
- Difficulty in activities requiring sequential processing, from the physical (such as dance steps) to the abstract (reading, writing, and signaling things in the right order). May have trouble even with a calculator due to difficulties in the process of feeding in variables.
- The condition may lead, in extreme cases, to a phobia of mathematics and mathematical devices.

THE MOST USELESS FACTS IN MATH

- If you multiply 1089 by 9, you get 9801. It's reversed itself! This also works with 10989, 109989, 1099989, and so on.
- 1 is the only positive whole number that you can add to 1,000,000 that gives you an answer that's greater than if you multiply it by 1,000,000.
- $19 = 1 \times 9 + 1 + 9$ and $29 = 2 \times 9 + 2 + 9$. This also works for 39, 49, 59, 69, 79, 89, and 99.
- 2 is the only number that gives the same result added to itself as it does multiplied by itself.
- If you multiply 21,978 by 4, it turns backward.
- There are 12,988,816 different ways to cover a chessboard with 32 dominoes.
- You can chop a big lump of cheese into a maximum of 93 pieces with 8 straight cuts.
- $1 \div 37 = 0.027027027\ldots$ and $1 \div 27 = 0.037037037\ldots$
- 8 is the only cubed number that is 1 less than a squared number.
- To multiply 10,112,359,550,561,797,752,808,988,764,044,943, 820,224,719 by 9 you just move the 9 at the very end up to the front.
- The number 4 is the only number in the English language that is spelled with the same number of letters as the number itself.
- $1 \times 9 + 2 = 11$, $12 \times 9 + 3 = 111$, $123 \times 9 + 4 = 1111$, and so on.

WHAT ARE THE ODDS?

Sociologists have found that individuals typically have around 150 people whom they regard as "close." Therefore, each of us typically has an entourage of around 23,000 "friends of a friend." Then say we have about five acquaintances for each close friend, the number swells to 600,000.

Fancy seeing you here! The chances of meeting someone on a train with whom you share an acquaintance are therefore surprisingly high: for the population in the United Kingdom, it's around 1 in 100. If you also include socioeconomic factors that boost the numbers of people from particular backgrounds traveling by train to particular destinations, the chances rise even higher. Take another "coincidence": discovering you share the same birthday as someone. How big a gathering of people do you think you'd need to get odds better than 50:50 that at least two shared the same birthday? As there are 365 possible birthdays, you might guess the answer to be about half of 365—about 180 people. In fact, you need just 23.

This is because you're not asking for a match between a specific birthday—say, April 12th. All you want is a match between any two birthdays and any two people. This reduces the numbers of people needed to produce the "coincidence." To find at least two people born on April 12th, you'd need more than 250 people to give odds better than 50:50. The less specific you are about what you want, the more likely coincidences become. There is another effect at work behind some coincidences. They often seem surprising because we mix up two different probabilities: (1) the chances of something interesting happening; and (2) the chances of something interesting happening *after it has been given many opportunities to occur.*

DO TRY THIS AT HOME

This is really strange. Try it! Get a calculator:

1. Key into the calculator the first three digits of your phone number (the exchange, not the area code).

2. Multiply by 80.
3. Add 1.
4. Multiply by 250.
5. Add the last four digits of your phone number.
6. Add the last four digits of your phone number again.
7. Subtract 250.
8. Lastly, divide by 2.

Is this your phone number?

Bibliography

Barrau, Aurelien. "Physics in the Multiverse." *International Journal of High-Energy Physics*, November 2007.

Barrow, John D., and Frank J. Tipler. *The Anthropic Cosmological Principle.* New York: Oxford University Press, 1986.

Belz-Merk, Dr. Martina. *Counseling and Help for People with Unusual Experiences a the Outpatient Clinic of the Psychological Institute at the University of Freiburg.* IGGP – Information and Counseling Services, January 2007.

Bolton, Alain de. *The Architecture of Happiness.* New York: Vintage International, 2008.

Boyle, David, and Anita Roddick. *Numbers.* White River Junction, Vermont: Chelsea Green Publishing, 2004.

Cheiro, Count Louis Hamon. *Cheiro's Book of Numbers.* London: Barrie & Jenkins, 1978.

Davies, Paul. *The Goldilocks Enigma: Why Is the Universe Just Right for Life?* New York: Mariner Books, 2008.

Dawkins, Richard. *The God Delusion.* New York: Houghton Mifflin, 2006.

Hahn, Thich Nhat. *Living Buddha, Living Christ.* New York: Riverhead Books, 2007.

Haughton, Brian. *Haunted Spaces, Sacred Places.* Franklin Lakes, New Jersey: New Page Books, 2008.

Hawking, Stephen. *A Brief History of Time.* New York: Bantam Dell Publishing Group, 1988.

Hayes, Michael. *The Hermetic Code in DNA: The Sacred Principles in the Ordering of the Universe.* Rochester, Vermont: Inner Traditions, 2008.

———. *The Infinite Harmony.* London: Weidenfeld & Nicholson, 1994.

Heath, Richard. *Sacred Number and the Origins of Civilization.* Rochester, Vermont: Inner Traditions, 2007.

Hieronimus, Robert. *The United Symbolism of America: Deciphering Hidden Meanings in America's Most Familiar Art, Architecture and Logos.* Franklin Lakes, New Jersey: New Page Books, 2008.

Ifrah, Georges. *The Universal History of Numbers: From Prehistory to the Invention of the Computer.* New York: John Wiley and Sons, 2000.

Joseph, Frank, and Laura Beaudoin. *Opening the Ark of the Covenant: The Secret Power of the Ancients, The Knights Templar Connection, and the Search for the Holy Grail.* Franklin Lakes, New Jersey: New Page Books, 2007.

Jung, Carl J. *Synchronicity: An Acausal Connecting Principle.* New York: Bollingen Foundation, 1960.

Kenyon, J. Douglas, et al. *Forbidden Religion: Suppressed Heresies of the West.* Rochester, Vermont: Bear & Co., 2006.

Kenyon, J. Douglas, et al. *Forbidden Science: From Ancient Technologies to Free Energy.* Rochester, Vermont: Bear & Co., 2006.

Kenyon, J. Douglas, et al. *Forbidden History: Prehistoric Technologies, Extraterrestrial Intervention and the Suppressed Origins of Civilization.* Rochester, Vermont: Bear & Co., 2005.

Kosminsky, Isidore. *Numbers: Their Meaning and Magic.* New York: Puttnam and Sons, 1927.

Lloyd, Seth. *Programming the Universe: A Quantum Computer Scientist Takes on the Cosmos.* New York: Vintage, 2006.

Malkowski, Edward F. *The Spiritual Technology of Ancient Egypt: Sacred Science and the Mystery of Consciouness.* Rochester, Vermont: Inner Traditions, 2007.

McTaggart, Lynne. *The Field: The Quest for the Secret Force in the Universe.* New York: HarperCollins, 2002.

Michell, John. *The Dimensions of Paradise: Sacred Geometry, Ancient Science and the Heavenly Order on Earth.* Rochester, Vermont: Inner Traditions, 2008.

Naudon, Paul. *The Secret History of Freemasonry—Its Origins and Connection to the Knights Templar.* Rochester, Vermont: Inner Traditions, 1991.

Peat, F. David. *Synchronicity: The Bridge Between Mind and Matter.* New York: Bantam New Age Books, 1987.

Rees, Martin. *Just Six Numbers: The Deep Forces That Shape the Universe.* New York: Basic Books, 2000.

Roberts, Courtney. *The Star of the Magi: The Mystery That Heralded the Coming of Christ.* Franklin Lakes, New Jersey: New Page Books, 2007.

Schwaller de Lubicz, R. A. *Sacred Science.* Rochester, Vermont: Inner Traditions, 1988.

Szalavitz, Maia. "Your Brain on Math." *Time Magazine*, April 23, 2013.

Talbot, Michael. *The Holographic Universe.* England: Grafton Books, 1991.

Voss, Sarah. *What Number Is God? Metaphors, Metaphysics, Metamathematics and the Nature of Things.* New York: State University of New York Press, 1995.

Watkins, Alfred. *The Old Straight Track: Its Mounds, Beacons, Moats, Sites and Mark Stones.* Glastonbury, United Kingdom: Lost Library, 2013.

Westcott, W. W. *Numbers: Their Occult Power and Mystic Virtue.* England: Theosophical Publishing House, reprint 1974.

About the Authors

Marie D. Jones has been involved with science, metaphysics, and the paranormal for most of her life, which led to a fascination with quantum physics and the writing of her popular and highly regarded book, *PSIence: How New Discoveries in Quantum Physics and New Science May Explain the Existence of Paranormal Phenomena.* Marie is also author of over fifteen books in print on the paranormal, metaphysics, consciousness, ancient knowledge, and unknown anomalies.

Marie began her extensive writing career as a teenager by writing movie and video reviews for a variety of national magazines, as well as short stories, including award-winning science fiction and speculative fiction for small press genre and literary magazines. She is now a widely published author with hundreds of credits to her name.

Her essays, articles, and stories have appeared in *Chicken Soup for the Working Woman's Soul, Chicken Soup to Inspire a Woman, If Women Ruled the World, God Allows U-Turns, UFO Magazine, The Book of Thoth, Paranormal Magazine, Light Connection Magazine, Alternate Realities, Unity Magazine, Whole Life Times, Science of Mind Magazine,* and many others.

Her background also includes more than fifteen years in the entertainment industry as a promotions assistant for Warner Bros. Records, film production assistant, and script reader for a variety of film and cable TV companies. She is now a full-time writer with two middle-grade novels debuting in 2018 and 2019. She is also an optioned screenwriter and has her own production company, "Where's Lucy? Productions."

In her capacity as an author and researcher, Marie has appeared at several major conferences, including CPAK and the Queen Mary Ghost Hunting Weekend. She has been interviewed on more than 100 radio talk shows including *Coast To Coast* with George Noory, NPR, KPBS Radio, Dreamland, and the *Shirley MacLaine Show*, and has been featured in dozens of newspapers, magazines, and online publications all throughout the world. She was also active with two MUFON groups during the 1990s as a field investigator.

She currently lives in San Diego, California, with her son, Max.

Larry Flaxman has been actively involved in paranormal research and hands-on field investigation for more than ten years and melds his technical, scientific, and investigative backgrounds together for no-nonsense, scientifically objective explanations regarding a variety of anomalous phenomena. He is the president and senior researcher of ARPAST, the Arkansas Paranormal and Anomalous Studies Team, which he founded in February 2007. Under his leadership, ARPAST has become one of the nation's largest and most active paranormal research organizations, with more than 150 members worldwide dedicated to conducting research into the paranormal using the most stringent scientific methodology. ARPAST is also now a proud member of the TAPS family (The Atlantic Paranormal Society). Larry supervises a staff of fully trained researchers and more than $250,000 worth of top-of-the-line equipment. Widely respected for his expertise on the proper use of equipment and techniques for conducting a solid investigation, Larry also serves as technical advisor to several paranormal research groups throughout the country.

Larry has appeared in numerous print interviews, including features in local and regional newspapers, magazines, and online publications such as *The Anomalist*, *Times Herald News*, *Jacksonville Patriot*, *ParaWeb*, *Current Affairs Herald*, *Unexplained Magazine*, and *The Pine Bluff Commercial*. He has been interviewed for several local and regional news television outlets such as *Ozarks First*, as well as national cable television, most recently appearing in a two-part special on ARPAST for MudTruck TV. He has been interviewed on dozens of radio programs, including *X-Zone*, *Ghostly Talk*, *Eerie Radio*, *Crossroads Paranormal*, *Binall of America*, and *Haunted Voices*.

Larry has authored several published articles regarding science and the paranormal, and is a regular columnist for *The Paranormal Awareness Society* newsletter. He is also cocreator (with Marie D. Jones) of *ParaExplorers.com*, devoted to the exploration of ancient and modern unknown mysteries, and is developing a line of related books and products. In addition, Larry is cocreator of the popular new ParaTracker software program for documenting data from paranormal investigations. His own ARPAST online research database system, SOCIUS, is considered one of the most comprehensive in the field. His enthusiasm for education and training in the paranormal field has also garnered many requests for special events and seminars, including popular charity investigations at haunted locations throughout the South, lectures on paranormal awareness for the Breckenridge Movie Theatre chain, and Teen Technology Night at the Nixon Library.

Larry also currently works in law enforcement/information technology. He is married and lives in Little Rock, Arkansas.